Junior
Show
Jumping

Introduction by Bertalan de Nemethy
Jumping Coach, U.S. Equestrian Team

Junior Show Jumping

Judy Crago

Thomas Y. Crowell Company
Established 1834 New York

Copyright © 1977 by Judy Crago

Produced by Walter Parrish International Limited, London

Designed by Roger Hyde

Printed and bound in Great Britain by Purnell and Sons Limited,
Paulton, near Bristol, Avon, England

Library of Congress Cataloging in Publication Data

Crago, Judy.
   Junior show jumping.
   Bibliography: p
   Includes index.
   SUMMARY: Discusses the basics of show jumping from buying
   and schooling a horse to competing at major shows.
      1. Show jumping.
   [1. Show jumping. 2. Horse shows] I. Title.
   SF295.5.C7   798'.25   77-102
   ISBN 0-690-01444-9

To the children's ponies,
Dougal, Dandy, and Zulu

Contents

Introduction

It is a human weakness, or perhaps an over-preoccupation with one's own interest, sometimes to overlook a talented performer until a big victory.

I have known Judy Crago for many years. We were at many shows in many places in Europe where 'my boys and girls' were often competing against her and she against us.

It takes no time for anyone to realize what a real, straightforward, down-to-earth human being Judy is, and certainly her sweetness and beauty must impress men and women equally from the first. But my admiration for her as a rider started when I saw the performance with Spring Fever that won her The Queen Elizabeth II Cup at White City.

Reading this book written by her about riding and horses reveals another Judy Crago. She is not only a charming, delightful, but nevertheless tough competitor of the International Show Jumping set; she is also a very able, competent, logical writer explaining step by step, for the young and for the older rider, what she was doing, what she is doing, and what is most advisable for others to do to succeed.

She puts the true, classical riding principles to training ponies, young and older horses in different circumstances, caring for them, or travelling with them, in a simple language as a guideline for beginners and to keep the more advanced on the right track. She does all this in a way that is easy to read, easy to remember and very enjoyable.

For me, who perhaps can claim some credit for the advanced and more sophisticated use of the so-called cavalletti and gymnastic work with jumpers, it is a special satisfaction to read her explanation of this kind of training and focusing her readers' attention on its importance.

I heartily recommend Judy Crago's book to riders of all ages, teachers of riding, and all those loving the horse sports. They will learn a lot from it and enjoy it, every chapter, as much as I did.

Bertalan de Nemethy

Preface

This is a book about show jumping. There have been hundreds of books on equitation, horsemanship and horsemastership, many of them including a chapter about jumping horses, but this book is specially dedicated to young riders, the people who are just starting out, who are willing and eager to begin show jumping and devote themselves to it whole-heartedly. The young are among the most important people in any sport, for they will be responsible for its future.

Show jumping is itself a young sport. Over the last thirty years it has grown from a small, select and little-known outdoor activity into one of the most popular international sports in Great Britain, Europe and America and all over the world. Competitions, indoors and outdoors, are held almost all the year round.

What sort of person is likely to succeed? The sport has grown to such gigantic proportions that it now demands full-time dedication, hours of long, hard work and countless personal sacrifices from those who are aiming at the top. And make no mistake, you must aim at the top. Without this burning ambition you will never succeed. But if you want it badly enough, work hard enough and have a little bit of luck on your side you will make it.

You must be resilient, no matter what your level of competition. Remember, there will be just as many knocks, disappointments and setbacks when you are competing at international level as when you begin, so you have to be prepared to take them as they come. Show jumping is one sport in which no person is always on top. In tennis, athletics, swimming, in fact in many other sports, each competitor is a single individual. In show jumping you have a partnership of two individuals, your horse and you. In order to win, this partnership must be in complete harmony and both of you must be one hundred per cent on form. There is also of course a certain amount of luck involved in every competition. It is these various factors which make the results of each class so unpredictable, and this is one of the main attractions of the sport, both from the spectator's point of view and from the competitor's.

With so much depending on the horse, and with good horses so hard to find, every rider at some time or another will find himself without a good mount. Even the best rider can look average on a moderate horse! This is another reason for you always to be willing to try, and do your best. No matter how strong the opposition, never go into a competition thinking you haven't a chance of winning. There again, a really good young rider can often coax a surprisingly good performance out .of a very ordinary horse. Almost anything can happen, particularly in novice classes! Of course, as you near the top of the tree, where courses become bigger and more demanding, the skill and experience of the rider may well have more bearing on the result than the ability of the horse. Over novice courses a good horse can carry a bad rider and get him out of trouble, but at more advanced levels the position of the big fences and the distance between them are set to test the rider's skill to the utmost.

There is no room for over-confidence or conceit in show jumping. You never know when disaster may be just round the corner. A rider can be right on form and having a fantastic run of luck, and then suddenly hit an unlucky patch of 'four-faultitis' or have a crashing fall. Every top rider knows the undignified feeling of being deposited among poles or in the middle of a water jump, watching his horse trot from the ring amid laughter from the crowd. You must always be able to laugh at yourself, and I am sure this is why there is so little jealousy and back-biting among the show-jumping fraternity.

Show jumping brings together a broad cross-section of the community. People from all parts of the world, from all walks of life, from exalted and humble background, are drawn together with one great thing in common—their love of the horse. In show jumping everyone is equal. When I retire I think that what I shall miss most of all is being an active member of this vast social community, the World of Show Jumping. It is a way of life, whether you are competing at a local unaffiliated show or in the vast arena of a C.S.I.O. (Concours de Saut International Officiel—an international show). It is a long, hard climb from the one to the other, but if you make it you will know the satisfaction of having succeeded against long odds!

A good start

1

Where do you start? We will assume that you have been riding for some time and that you have some basic knowledge of equitation and horsemastership. A very few of you may be lucky enough to come from a 'horsey' background, with a number of ponies to ride. The chances are, however, that most of you will have long-suffering parents who are willing—perhaps even eager—to help you to achieve your ambitions, but are not sure what to do about it. My advice is to start on a horse or pony who is

Pony Clubs provide the opportunity to compete in many phases of riding. Here is a typical Pony Club cross-country fence.

experienced and knows his job. One who has been around, and has travelled the shows with different children, is an ideal teacher. It may be an old top-grade pony which is past competing in recognized, or 'affiliated', shows, or one which has been jumped only in Pony Club and unaffiliated shows and therefore has no official winnings credited to him—either way it does not matter as it is these small shows which will give you your first taste of competition.

While it is good experience to ride as many different types of pony or horse as possible if you get the chance, take my advice and keep off the ones that stop! There is nothing like riding a 'stopper' to ruin your confidence, capability and enthusiasm, particularly at this vulnerable stage of your career.

When choosing your first jumper you should, if possible, take your instructor with you. If you have no instructor as yet, then find someone experienced in show jumping who knows you well, not only as a rider but also as a personality. You want someone who understands equine temperament, too, and who can assess a horse's physical and mental qualities. Take his advice, even if it means passing up a horse or pony you like. Just keep looking around until you're both satisfied.

It is impossible to give general advice on price. The exact figure depends on any number of things—age, ability, potential or experience, conformation and, of course, how keen the owner is to sell. While it is impossible to pick a show jumper on his conformation, it is obviously better to choose a reasonably well-made animal if he is untried. A horse which is well put together and has natural balance is *more likely* to make a show jumper, but if he doesn't then you will find him easier to sell as a hunter or eventer. Negotiation, or 'horse trading', is an accepted part of buying any animal.

The suitability of your jumper to you as a rider is also something I cannot advise on here, as each rider is different and every horse or pony is different. I would not suggest that young people buy anything unbroken, but, aside from that, an animal which may be ideal for one person will not necessarily suit others, even if their riding is of the same standard. This is where personalities come into it. A highly strung, nervous type of pony is better suited to the placid, even-tempered child, while the rider who is temperamental or lacks confidence will get on

The author riding Spring Fever, the horse on which she won the Queen Elizabeth II Cup.

better with a quiet pony. Strength is another important factor. Many people aged twelve or thirteen are not strong enough to manage a strong animal without over-bitting.

Basically, the experienced horse or pony is the best proposition for the beginner, as you will learn little from a novice at this stage, and he will learn less from you.

Your education during these early formative days will lay the foundation upon which to build your future riding career. For this reason it is vital that you should get enough practice in as many different kinds of riding as possible. This is the grounding for your becoming a horseman, and any habits, good or bad, which form now will quickly become second nature.

During this period the Pony Club can play an important role. It can provide you with instruction in dressage, cross-country and show jumping, as well as stable-management, together with an opportunity to compete in all these phases. Many Pony Clubs are lucky enough to have excellent instructors, while others have to rely on anyone who is willing and able. Remember, you will always learn by listening and watching, and while some of what you see and hear may not agree with what you have already learned, by sifting through the information you will be able to store in your mind what you need and discard the rest.

One thing is certain—you will need help, so do not try and 'go it alone'. If possible you should try to find a good instructor before you acquire too many bad habits. This does not necessarily mean someone with a lot of letters after his name. Experience is the best teacher, so it follows that the best instructors are those with practical experience of what they are teaching. If you want to show-jump you cannot do better than go to someone who has himself achieved success in this field. There are any number of ways to find an instructor. Personal recommendation is the best way, although some instructors advertise in equestrian periodicals and you could follow up one of these —but do try and find out from other sources whether they are any good or not. In the US you may see notices advertising instructors in Riding Academies or tack shops. Ask around at the shows, and make enquiries from the people who know. Some trainers, it should be noted, command top fees, but this does not necessarily mean they are any good. Furthermore, they may require that you own an expensive, top-flight horse.

When competitors in the Pony Club Games are so carried away in their enthusiasm and eagerness to win, it is often their ponies who suffer. Here the rider in the middle is being rough with her hands, and the pony is looking very uncomfortable and distressed.

Whoever you select, it's a good idea to take a trial lesson or observe several of his schooling sessions. Like your horse, your instructor's temperament will have a bearing on your progress and appreciation of the sport.

At this early stage, as I have already said, you should try to gain experience in as many different forms of riding as possible. One exception to this, in my opinion, is the Pony Club Mounted Games. I say this with some reservations because I know these Games give immense pleasure to countless numbers of children in Britain, and may also improve a young rider's confidence, balance and agility. Certainly, too, the Games foster a tremendous competitive spirit among those taking part and their supporters, and this spirit is essential for winning competitions. But we will assume that you are already blessed with the will to win, without which you will certainly never succeed in show jumping. My objection to these Games is that the riders taking part do tend to get carried away in their enthusiasm and eagerness to win, and to forget the finer points of the art of riding! So perhaps this is one sort of experience to avoid.

The hunting field is an excellent schooling ground for both the young rider and the young horse. I am sure that the success of the British riders over the last few years has been largely due to their experience in the hunting field. Unfortunately this sort of riding will not be so easily available to American or Australian readers, although many Pony Clubs and other organizations include hunting as part of their activities. Riding regularly across country over natural obstacles will help you to develop your natural sense of *balance* and *rhythm*. This is what show jumping is all about. Throughout this book I will stress the importance of timing, and of being able to see a stride and adjust it without losing this essential balance and rhythm. Some riders have a natural 'eye', others can acquire it to a certain degree with practice, and those of you who are lucky enough to have two or three horses or ponies to ride will have the advantage here. If you have only one animal obviously you should not jump him every time you go out for a ride (he will not last long if you do!) but you can practise 'seeing a stride' by picking out objects on the

Riding across country is a marvellous education for horse and rider. It gives the horse confidence and the ability to handle himself and it helps the rider to develop a sense of balance and rhythm. Here you can see how a horse learns to accept natural obstacles without fuss or excitement.

ground as you canter along, and shortening or lengthening your stride as you go.

You really do need help and instruction right from the start. This has nothing to do with how good or bad you are. In fact every show-jumping rider, novice or experienced, needs somebody 'on the ground' to correct faults from time to time. While it is all too easy to see another rider's mistakes from the ground it is always extremely difficult to sort out your own problems from the saddle. It is only since I met Brian, my husband, that I have realized the importance of having someone on the ground to help you, and I now wonder how I ever managed without. Certainly, I did run into trouble fairly often, and I used to pick the brains of all the established riders until they must have been sick to death of me.

Find a good instructor before you get into too many bad habits. If there are two or three of you in the same class, you will learn a lot from listening and watching him correcting the others and seeing the effect on what they do.

Never be afraid to ask. Listen to everything you are told. Go to as many shows as you can, and watch every horse and every rider jump every fence. Try to analyse why each mistake is made, and if you can't work it out *ASK*. You will find the top riders are only too willing to help a young rider who is keen to learn, so listen to everything they say and digest every bit of information. Some of the opinions may vary, but you can always learn from listening to other people's comments. Watch the top riders closely not only in show jumping, but also in dressage and eventing, for these are top horsemen. Once you become an accomplished horseman you will find it easier to adapt yourself to different types of horse in whichever sphere you choose. Remember, though, that show jumping *is* a specialist field, and not all that you learn at this stage will necessarily apply later on when you concentrate on your show jumping seriously. This is why I stressed earlier the importance of having a good instructor who is experienced in show jumping.

In Pony Club instruction you may well be told things from time to time which many of the show-jumping riders would disagree with. For example, you will frequently be told 'not to kick'. Just how strongly you must use your legs

will depend on your pony. A lazy horse or pony or a nappy one will need very strong leg aids and you will *have* to kick it unless you want to stand there all day! This will also apply to a young, green animal. This does not mean that you have to keep flapping your legs—when a squeeze has no effect give him a firm kick and if necessary use a stick at the same time.

Another thing you will often hear in the Pony Club is 'never hit your pony'. Now obviously you should never lose your temper and hit animals needlessly, but, like children, they have to learn obedience, and an undisciplined pony is not a happy one. You must correct your horse if he does wrong, but hit him hard, immediately and not five minutes later, and then leave him alone. Never hit a pony on bony parts of his anatomy or anywhere around his head—you are administering more a psychological than a physical reprimand. Always make sure that he understands what you are trying to tell him. The horse is a very willing pupil with a very good memory, so correct him firmly when he is wrong and reward him when he does well, and he will learn quickly.

'Give him the reins as he takes off' is another great favourite! In other words, 'Throw your hands up his neck

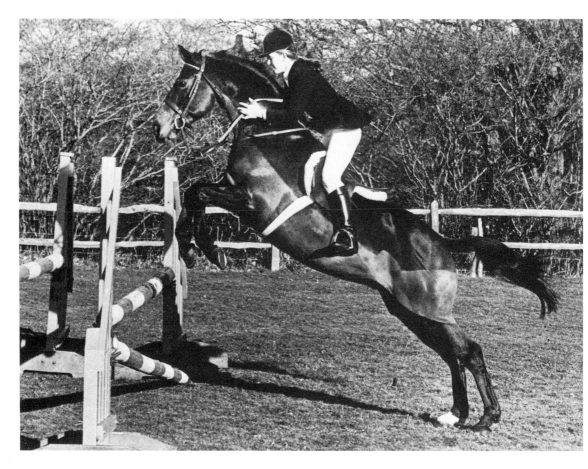

Taking off: this is what you should *not* do. Here the rider is standing upon take-off and not only letting the horse's head go, but also opening her fingers and letting the reins slip through them. When she lands it will take two or three strides before she regains control and balance.

and drop his head'—believe me this is the *last* thing you want to do! Admittedly there are a few top riders who successfully adopt this method (Caroline Bradley is one of them) but they have perfected the technique to a fine art, and it would be extremely foolish to try to copy them. Their horses are invariably beautifully schooled, ultra-obedient and perfectly balanced. In order to allow a horse to jump with his head completely free it is essential to place him with complete accuracy at every fence, and to have him perfectly balanced between your legs, hands and weight, and to do this successfully requires years of experience.

Another method at the other extreme used by some of the experts, to 'lift' a horse's head as he takes off, is an even more dangerous practice for the novice rider as the horse tends to throw his head up, stiffen his neck and jump with a hollow back. The ideal is to keep an even feel of the horse's mouth throughout the approach and the jump, but never to lose contact.

Many riding instructors who teach only the basic principles of show jumping favour the method of 'non-intervention' in the approach to a fence, leaving the horse to make his own arrangements. This may be both stylish and effective at novice level when courses are small and the distances between fences straightforward. However, as you progress to a more advanced level, accuracy becomes more and more important and precision of stride is essential. This is why it is important to bear in mind that some of the things you will be taught in your early Pony Club days will not necessarily apply in advanced show jumping.

So listen to everything you are told, and if you don't agree with it don't argue! Remember everybody is entitled to his own opinion, and each individual has his own methods which may be extremely successful—there are no hard and fast rules about horses because no two animals are alike; but you must follow some sort of pattern, so once you have found a good instructor who knows about *show jumping*, stick to him and follow his advice.

To sum up, keep your ears and eyes open, and gain as much experience as you can on as many different ponies and in as many different branches of the sport as possible, but do not forget that your ultimate aim is to become a top-class *show jumper.*

Compare this take-off with the one shown opposite: here the rider has gone to the other extreme, not allowing her pony enough freedom of head and neck to extend himself over the fence. She is too far forward and is balancing herself by leaning on the reins.

Balance is the key

2

I do not believe in trying to force all people into the same style of riding, since individuality and flair are important in the make-up of sportsmen in any field. I think all riders should be allowed to develop their own little peculiarities and it is a mistake to try and change them. Certainly the top show-jumping riders of the world have very different styles of riding, all of which are extremely successful. But, as I have already said, show jumping is a partnership of two individuals, and the horse and the rider must be in complete harmony and perfectly balanced. You will have heard people say, 'So-and-so is at one with his horse', and this is what the partnership should be—a union of horse and rider. As I said before, and will repeat again and again, balance is the key to show jumping, and the position of the rider is obviously important in maintaining balance.

The horse's balance will be disturbed if the rider's weight moves about; therefore this weight must always be over the point of the centre of gravity, on an imaginary line running through the deepest point of a horse's back. The line of the centre of gravity should pass straight through the rider's shoulder, hip and heel. The aids must be co-ordinated with this centre of gravity and should be adjusted with the movement of the horse.

The rider should sit deep into the saddle in a natural, relaxed position. The best way to achieve this is by spending many hours on the lunge without stirrups—an exhausting business but very good for your riding, and for developing a deep, firm seat. Take care that your position does not become too rigid. You must be relaxed and supple at all times. Riding without stirrups will also help to improve your balance, and safeguard against the day when you have a stirrup break in the ring. I remember seeing Harvey Smith jumping Farmer's Boy, the horse on

A good position. The rider is sitting deep in the saddle with her weight in the right place; her hands are carried properly with thumbs up; her body is relaxed.

The centre of gravity should be on a line passing through the rider's shoulder, hip and heel, and through the deepest point of the horse's back.

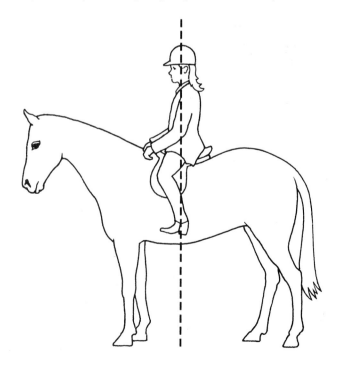

which he first gained his reputation, in the puissance class at the British Timken Show years ago. His girth broke half way round the course, and Harvey slid the saddle out behind him and continued without it. It didn't make the slightest difference to his accuracy, and he finished with a clear round! Harvey demonstrated his marvellous balance once again when he was riding Salvador in the Hickstead Derby of 1975. His stirrup leather broke when he was coming into the 'road' fence, number seven. This is one of the many permanent obstacles in the International Arena at Hickstead. It is a 'table' type bank with a ditch behind a rail going onto the bank, then three strides to another ditch before the rail going off the bank. Harvey's leather broke when he was within two or three strides of the fence so that Salvador was for a moment unbalanced to jump the first part, and they had the rail down. But the pair immediately recovered and finished the rest of the long and difficult course without further fault.

The one point of the rider's body which should always be in contact with the horse is the knee, and it is on the knee that your weight should pivot with the movement of the horse. Your knee should always be in the same place and not move backwards or forwards. The lower leg must always be in a position to command the horse, as this forms an important part of the aids. It should not be thrown backwards or forwards over a fence as movement here will tend to upset the rider's whole balance. The leg should be kept constantly against the ribs of the horse, with the foot in a relaxed position, facing forward, with the toes up. The stirrup should be under the ball of the foot, and not right 'home' under the instep. The knee and ankle must be supple and relaxed, as stiffness in any part of the body will tend to spread through the body. This is why you must not be such a slave to position that you have to force yourself into an unnatural shape! If you are made in such a way that you find it uncomfortable to adopt the 'classical' position then just try and sit as naturally as you can. Remember that as long as you are sitting comfortably you are more likely to be relaxed.

So, although the top riders' styles may vary to a large degree, the position in the saddle is important in that it must affect the horse's balance. The seat should be firm but at the same time supple, for suppleness is essential to balance. A good saddle is important to ensure that you sit in the centre and lowest part, and this will allow for

Harvey Smith jumping Salvador in the 1975 British Jumping Derby after his stirrup leather had broken when coming into the seventh fence. He finished this gruelling course without further fault, so emphasizing the importance of a deep, independent seat, and perfect balance.

varying the lengths of your stirrup leathers without affecting the position of your seat.

Your seat should be entirely independent of the reins, and there are some good exercises to perfect this. These exercises should be done on the lunge on a quiet horse or pony. To start with, they should be performed for short periods only, as they can be very tiring at first, but as your muscles get used to the exercises, you will find them easier. All the exercises should be done without reins and stirrups, and, with the exception of the first one, first at the walk and later at the trot.

1. Sitting trot without stirrups. This is a good exercise for getting the rider to sit deep in the saddle, and for developing a strong, independent seat.

2. Turn the toes round in circles, first one way and then the other, and do the same with the hands. This is a good suppling exercise for the ankles and the wrists.

3. Keeping your arms straight, stretch them out sideways until they are at right-angles with your body, then forwards in front of your nose, and back again, and then raise them above your head. Repeat several times, and then vary the exercise by drawing your hands back under your chin with elbows bent and level with your shoulders. Push your elbows back as far as you can two or three times while still keeping your hands under your chin. Finally throw your arms out straight again.

Above: For the novice rider the sitting trot without stirrups on the lunge is a very good exercise, developing a strong independent seat. The experienced rider, too, should go back to this exercise from time to time to correct his position. The rider here is in a good relaxed position.

Opposite, top and bottom: The arm exercises described in this chapter will improve your balance and supple your neck, shoulders and back. They will help you to develop an independent seat and improve your sense of rhythm and co-ordination. It is important to keep a correct seat and leg position. In both the photographs the rider has stiffened the lower leg and ankle and is gripping with her heels instead of her knees.

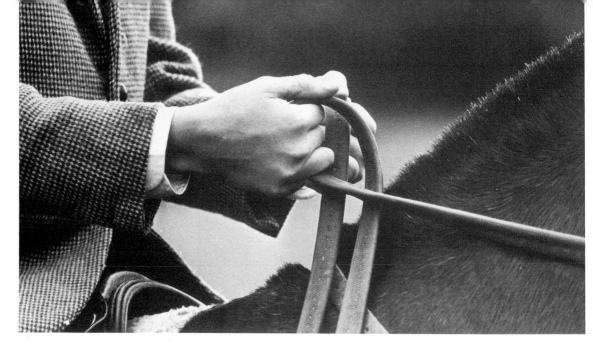

The reins should be held firmly between the three middle fingers and the thumb. The wrist should be supple at all times to maintain the line of communication.

4. Swing the arms backwards alternately in a circular motion, keeping the body and the head in an upright, relaxed position, so that the movement of the arms comes from the shoulders only. All these arm exercises will supple your back, neck and shoulders and improve your balance.

5. Raise the arms above the head and then touch your toes with both hands together, first one side and then the other. Take great care to bend only from the hips so that your seat remains in the saddle and your legs in the same position.

6. Bend your body forwards and then backwards from the waist, until horizontal.

7. With your arms outstretched turn your body from the waist, first one way and then the other, making sure that your seat and legs do not move. Repeat several times.

8. Rise from the saddle and then sit gently without bumping as if doing a rising trot.

During all these exercises your body should remain supple and relaxed while keeping the correct position in the saddle.

To return to your position: your arms should hang down naturally to the elbows, which should be close to the body in front of the hips. The forearms should form a straight line through the reins to the horse's mouth.

The hands are probably the most important part of your contact with the horse. My small daughter Felicity discovered this early on. Riding her first small, woolly pony at the age of five, she was having trouble with the steering. He would keep turning round in a wide circle (he was much too nice to spin round quickly) and trotting back to where Brian and I were standing. We explained to her that if she pulled the right rein he would turn right, and if she pulled the left rein he would turn left. So she tried it. To her surprise and delight it worked, and as she trotted away she called out, 'Gosh! Don't these reins come in handy'—a great discovery! But to return to the finer points, this communication from the rider's hands to the horse's mouth through the reins is particularly important in top-class show jumping, when instant obedience from the horse is essential. David Broome, who is in my opinion the greatest rider in the world, has an exceptionally light pair of hands, and can adjust his horse's stride with the slightest touch without in any way interfering with the balance and rhythm. The hands should be carried with the thumbs uppermost, and your fingers and wrists should be supple enough to follow the movement of the horse, and to maintain an even feel on his mouth. It is through the reins that you direct the horse and regulate his pace, and your hands must be responsive so that you can 'give' and 'take' immediately. With a well-schooled horse only the slightest movement will be needed. As soon as he responds to a tightening of the reins you should relax the pressure; then if he shows signs of resistance, you will be ready to tighten your fingers and hold him until he relaxes again. When a horse resists in the mouth, his whole body will become stiff, so it is essential that he should relax his lower jaw and flex from the poll when asked.

Remember, though, that only one hand should 'ask' while the other retains an even contact with the horse's mouth. Never pull continuously on both reins as he will only lean on the bit and pull harder.

It may sound complicated, but the co-ordination of the aids—hands, legs and weight—will come with practice. Like balance and rhythm, this is something that you will come to *feel* with experience. Your hands should be used in conjunction with your weight and your legs, but entirely independently of your seat, and you must *never* use the reins to maintain your balance and position.

Of course, with a young horse or pony your aids will have to be considerably more exaggerated, but you must always be clear, precise and consistent in your demands so that he understands exactly what is asked of him.

Schooling on the flat

3

Whatever type of horse or pony you choose, you will need to have a good basic knowledge of 'schooling on the flat'. You may have a young, unschooled animal, or an old-stager who has developed some bad habits; or you may even be lucky enough to have one that is beautifully schooled. No matter which, your flat work should be an important part of your daily routine throughout your career.

This does *not* mean you have to spend hours every day

riding in circles; that would be exhausting and monotonous for both horse and rider. You can have a change from concentrated flat work, taking enjoyable rides in the countryside while still applying the basic principles of dressage. Do not be put off by the word 'dressage'—it covers a vast field and is not limited to riders who carry out those advanced movements within the white boards of the dressage arenas.

Some training on the flat is essential to every horse, whether he goes eventing, show jumping, hunting or even racing; it will develop his balance, improve his performance and make him supple and obedient. With a young horse it will help his physical and mental development and with an older one it will help to keep him responsive and alert. Watch the top international riders at work on the morning of a big show or warming up in the collecting ring before a class, and you will see them applying various degrees of dressage constantly; this must surely be proof of its value to a show jumper.

We will assume that your horse has been broken in—I do not advise you to buy anything unbroken. Your aim is to command complete obedience at all times; you must not let him get away with even the slightest disobedience. Give him his aids clearly every time, so that he doesn't get confused. Make sure that you are always quite consistent in your demands so that he understands what you want him to do.

Obedience starts right from the beginning—when you mount. First of all the horse must learn to stand quite still while you get on and not fidget around or try to walk off as soon as you put your foot in the stirrup. There is nothing more embarrassing than hopping round in circles in the ring, trying to remount a horse you have just fallen off while the spectators are laughing their heads off! Make him stand until you have both feet in the irons and are sitting comfortably. This might sound like fussing over minor details but your horse is learning that all-important obedience in each small lesson. Standing the horse so that his offside is close to a wall or fence will give him less of a chance to swing away.

Before giving an aid make sure that he is correctly balanced and in a position to answer that aid. When you are both ready, give him a clear signal with legs, weight (through your seat) and hands to move forward smoothly into a walk. Straighten your back, close both legs and

The pony is standing quietly and obediently while the rider mounts.

maintain a light contact with his mouth. He should not be allowed to throw his head up and come 'off the bit'. A young horse must first learn to go forward, even if he goes on his forehand at first, in which case he may lean on the bit. Do not try to pull his head up with your hands as he will only become heavier. Once he is going forward then you can push his hindquarters up with your weight and legs while keeping a firm contact with his mouth. If he throws his head up he will come off the bit, hollow his back and leave his hocks behind him. It is much harder to correct a horse which comes behind the bit, but the same principles apply and you must use your legs and weight to push him forward.

This is a typical example of a pony going on his forehand. His hocks are out behind him and he is leaning on the bit.

Here the rider has tried to push the horse's hind quarters up with her weight and legs. Too strong pressure with the hands has caused the horse to resist. He is throwing his head up to evade the bit and hollowing his back.

There are various ways in which a horse can evade the bit. He can put his tongue over the bit or draw his tongue back behind it. A horse which leans on the bit is said to be 'over the bit'. If he raises his head and takes the pressure of the bit on his lips instead of on the bars of the mouth he is 'above the bit'. Finally, a horse is 'behind the bit' if he drops it and brings his mouth back towards his chest. When his head remains in the correct position according to his pace, his hocks are under him, and he offers no resistance to a light contact with his mouth, then he is 'on the bit'.

It is essential that you are always in a position to influence and control your horse's hindquarters as, while he is using these correctly, he will not be on his forehand As you push his hocks under him, his hind legs will come closer to the centre of gravity and the forehand will become freer and more relaxed; you should be able to keep your horse on the bit at all paces so that he is balanced and in a position to answer your aids.

His paces at all times should be regulated to a steady rhythm and cadence. The walk should be an easy, natural movement with four regular beats.

The trot is a pace of two-time—a movement of the two diagonals in turn; the right diagonal is the off-foreleg and the near-hind, and the left diagonal the near-fore and the off-hind. When trotting in a circle, the rider should rise with the outside diagonal, that is, as the outside foreleg comes forward. When the horse's inside hind leg comes to the ground, this is his supporting leg and it is therefore easier for him to balance himself if the rider's weight comes down on this leg. This also applies when trotting in a straight line, as even then your flexion will be on one rein, the 'inside' rein, while the 'outside' rein retains an

A good, regular walk, with the horse balanced and on the bit.

A free and active trot, with the horse's hocks engaged; the head is slightly too high because the rider's hands are fixed.

even contact. Varying the diagonals while trotting in a straight line is a good way to exercise a horse's back, loins, and quarters, but make sure you vary your flexion at the same time. This is one of the many useful exercises you can do while out for a ride. A horse is usually more comfortable on one diagonal than the other as most horses are stiff on one side. By varying your diagonals in this way you will help to develop the muscles on the stiff side.

The trot should be free and active and full of impulsion, the driving force from the hind legs that moves the horse forwards. The position of the rider should be the same as at the walk, but just slightly ahead of the vertical to allow for the slight increase in pace. The rising movement should be forward down, forward down, ideally with ten per cent of the rider's weight supported in the stirrup, fifty per cent on the knee (which at all times should remain still) and the other forty per cent distributed along the thigh to the hip.

Let's now move on to the canter. The canter is a pace of three-time. The sequence when leading on the inside leg is as follows: outside hind, outside diagonal, inside fore, then outside hind again, and so on. With practice you will be able to feel which leg is leading without having to look down. You will also feel if your horse is disunited, that means leading with the near-fore and the off-hind or vice versa. This is very uncomfortable for the rider—and the easiest way to correct it is to pull the horse back to a trot and start again.

To ask for a canter on the correct leg, sit deep in your saddle, with your weight on your outside seat bone, bend the horse's head to the inside and use both legs—the outside one behind the girth and the inside one on the girth. The rider's outside leg should control the quarters and stop them swinging out while the inside leg ensures sufficient impulsion and dictates the length of the stride and the rhythm. The outside hand is the one that controls the pace and maintains an even feel on the horse's mouth while the inside hand regulates the amount of turn and asks for the flexion. The movement of the inside hand should be slightly sideways, away from the horse's shoulder, and not backwards, which would slow him up and interfere with his impulsion.

The transition to the halt from any movement should be quite smooth. Sitting deep into your saddle, brace your back slightly and squeeze gently with both legs while closing your fingers on the reins. Do not allow your horse to step back. He must stand straight and motionless with his weight evenly distributed over all four legs until you are ready to move off again.

The rein back is a backwards walk in two-time. As in the trot, it is an alternate movement of the two diagonals. Push the horse's hindquarters under him with your weight and your legs while at the same time keeping an even pressure on his mouth so that he cannot move forward. When he steps back one pace, relax the hands then repeat the aids. The horse should move back in a straight line—you must use your legs to stop his quarters swinging from side to side.

These are the basic elementary movements on the flat. You may feel that they are not very exciting in comparison with the show-jumping success you are aiming for—but don't be fooled into rushing ahead too fast with your training. These simple movements lay the foundations of success in the long run, and you must be able to do them properly before you try any form of jumping. Later on

A good halt. The rider is in a good position to give any necessary aid.

you will progress to more advanced movements on the flat—such as collected and extended paces, and turns on the forehand and hindquarters—all of which are good training for the horse, giving him the suppleness and obedience that every show jumper must have.

Once you have your horse moving forward freely, then the next stage is to teach him to answer your legs and your weight in co-ordination with your hands and to introduce him to work on two tracks and turns on the spot. The first and easiest of these movements is the turn on the forehand. This should only be done from the halt and the horse must stand square. Using your outside leg you must push your horse's quarters around his inside foreleg in a half-circle. To ask for a right turn on the forehand keep an even restraint on both reins to stop him moving forward. His head should be bent slightly to the right, your weight remains central and your right leg is used behind the girth to push his quarters around the off-

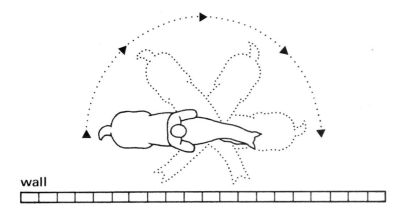

wall

foreleg, which acts as a pivot. Your left leg remains on the girth to prevent him from moving backwards. The right hind leg should cross in front of the left hind leg with an even, regular step, and you should walk your horse forward as soon as you have completed the movement.

Having gained control of the quarters in this way you will be ready to progress to the turn on the haunches. This should be done from a walk, starting initially with a small half-circle so that the horse is turning his whole body around his hind legs without the quarters slowing down. Throughout this movement he should maintain impulsion without moving backwards or sideways. This is a particularly important exercise for a jumper, as he must have his hocks under him at all times, and be able to make tight turns without losing impulsion.

To turn to the right, lead the forehand round with the right rein while the left retains an even contact; use your left leg behind the girth to stop the quarters swinging to the left and your right leg on the girth to prevent him from stepping backwards. The left foreleg must cross in front of the right foreleg while the inside right hind leg marks time.

Leg-yielding is a test of obedience and of the horse's willingness to move his hindquarters away from your leg. It is a preliminary exercise leading up to your more advanced movements on two tracks. In leg-yielding your horse has to move in a forward and sideways direction with his head bent in the opposite direction to which he is going. Use your inside leg to influence the horse's inside hind leg in rhythm with the movement.

With the shoulder-in he is again bent away from where he is going, but he must be sufficiently collected to be able to bring his inside hind leg directly under his centre of

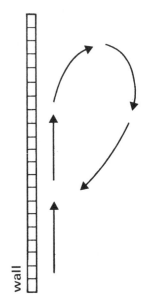

wall

For a right turn on the haunches, start initially with a small half-circle.

gravity. He should be bent round the rider's inside leg, the degree of the bend depending on the suppleness and obedience of the horse. With the shoulder-in he must bend in the body while going forward in a straight line. With leg-yielding his legs must cross as he moves forward diagonally.

The aim of the work on two tracks is to supple and flex the horse in the ribs and back, and this is important in the training of a show jumper. In a half-pass the horse moves on two tracks with his body bent in the direction he is going, giving more freedom of movement to the outside shoulder, with his forelegs and hind legs crossing each other. The head, neck and shoulders should always be slightly in advance of the quarters.

To commence your half-pass come out of the corner doing one or two steps of shoulder-in to bend the horse in the right direction. Leading with the inside rein, sit with your inside shoulder and hip in the same direction while the outside leg moves the horse sideways. As the hind leg leaves the ground the rider's leg should influence it as described in the next chapter (page 50). Keep enough pressure on the outside rein to prevent the horse turning but allow him to go forward.

Later on this exercise can be performed at the trot. The pace must remain even and if the exercise is performed across the diagonal of the school, the horse must remain parallel to the long side of the school. This work on two tracks should be attempted only after your horse has

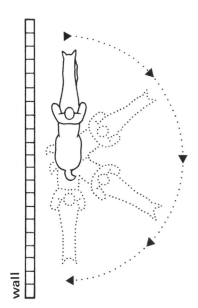

The right turn on the haunches.

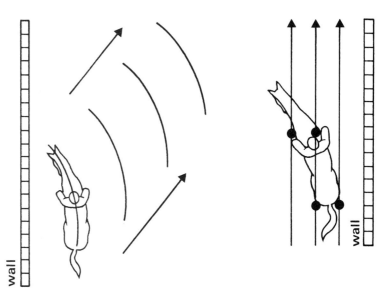

Right: Leg-yielding.

Far right: The shoulder-in.

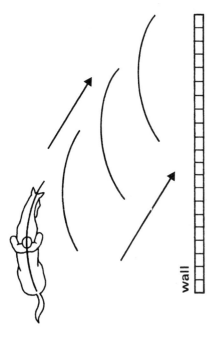

The half-pass.

Cantering in a serpentine.

learned obediently and accurately to perform the more simple movements, leg-yielding and shoulder-in.

Having now gained full control of the forehand and quarters, you can start to control your horse's stride. There are four recognized paces at the trot and canter —working, medium, extended and collected. The working trot, which used to be called the ordinary trot, is a pace between the extended and collected trot. The horse should move forward freely and straight with the rider maintaining a light but firm contact with his mouth. The stride should be regular and even with the hind feet stepping in the tracks of the front feet. The rhythm and length of stride of the medium trot is slightly in advance of the working trot, and in the extended trot he should cover as much ground as possible. The horse should remain on the bit with his neck extended, using his shoulders, with his hocks following through behind with great impulsion.

You should be able to execute these forward movements sufficiently well before attempting any collected work. The collected trot is a more active movement with a shorter stride but nevertheless great impulsion must be maintained to bring his hocks under him. The horse's head should be carried higher than in the extended paces with his neck flexed and bent at the poll. The same principles apply with the canter, and having gained the necessary impulsion in the working, medium, and extended canter, you can bring the horse back to the collected canter.

It is essential for a show jumper to be able to execute a flying change of leg ('lead') at the canter. This must become second nature to him so he must learn to do it without any fuss or excitement. Make it easy for him to

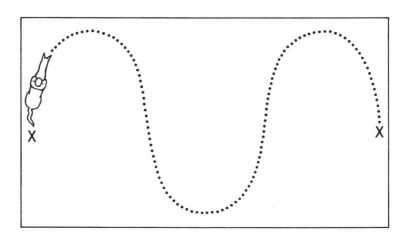

A half-pass to the right being performed as a collected trot. Notice how the horse is bent around the rider's inside leg.

A classic example of an extended trot. Notice how the horse's hind leg is coming well forward under the centre of gravity.

start with by teaching him the simple change, that is by bringing him back to the trot for a few steps before leading off on the other leg. To ask for a lead on the off-fore, bend the horse's head slightly to the right, sit deep in the saddle, especially with your left seat bone, and apply the left leg behind the girth and the right leg on the girth. You can then progress to cantering in serpentines, making your loops large to start with and bringing him back to a trot before each change of direction. Gradually you can make your trot strides fewer and your loops smaller. A show jumper has to change legs ('leads') several times during the course of a round, which he must be able to do without loss of balance or impulsion.

Starting to jump

4

As with your schooling on the flat, your work with trotting poles and cavalletti should be part of your regular routine, not only with a young horse or pony but right through your jumping career. This work is very good physical and mental exercise for both horse and rider; it improves a horse's balance, rhythm and co-ordination and helps to keep him alert and interested in his work.

Cavalletti work, including work with trotting poles, is an

excellent disciplined exercise requiring the use of all the important muscles in a horse's movement—it is invaluable in the development of these muscles. It helps in other ways too. Riding through cavalletti will help to relax and loosen up any stiffness which may result from over-tiredness or incorrect use of certain muscles. It also proves very effective in settling an excitable horse. It discourages him from rushing his fences and he will learn to accept that jumping is a natural and normal part of his routine. Work with cavalletti is also an essential part of the rider's training. You will find it a very useful exercise for improving your balance while maintaining your position, and for developing your concentration, your sense of stride and your feel for the horse's movements.

Let's start with trotting poles. The correct use of trotting poles will enable you to regulate your horse's stride; you will soon learn to adjust it, that is to shorten or lengthen it, without losing your essential rhythm. Take it gradually. With a young, green horse or pony you will begin by *walking* him over a single pole on the ground a few times. You can then place another pole about three feet away from the first, and then another and so on until you have from six to eight poles in a row. The exact distances between the poles will, of course, depend on the size and action of your horse or pony. A good average for a pony is 4 ft 6 in (1.37 m) to 4 ft 9 in (1.45 m) between the poles. When he is walking quietly over these without any fuss or excitement, you can start to *trot* him over a single pole, adjusting his stride so that his back legs step at equal

Above: Walking through poles. Both pony and rider are relaxed and the pony's hocks are well under him.

Right: A good active trot through poles. Notice how the poles are regulating the pony's rhythm so that he is stepping at an equal distance from each pole.

distances on each side of the pole. Keep him in a regular working trot and when you have an even rhythm and are able to adjust his stride over a single pole, then place another, and another, as before.

Let him go on a good length of rein without losing contact so that he can stretch his neck and look where he's going, but do not let him 'run'; he should move at a steady pace without trying to hurry. At first he will lack co-ordination and he will lift his front feet too high and trip with his back ones or vice versa. Soon, however, his balance will improve, his muscles will develop and he will become more supple and agile. His limbs will become more co-ordinated and he will settle into a good rhythmic stride with his hocks coming under him. He should continue on in this same rhythm each time after going down through the trotting poles.

The experienced rider will be able to stay in balance and rhythm at a sitting trot through the poles, but the novice rider will find it easier to do a rising trot, keeping plenty of weight on the knee with the hips moving forward as the body rises. Your lower legs should be kept against the horse, your hands carried to keep an even contact with his mouth (there should be a straight line from your elbows, through your hands to your horse's mouth) and your body slightly ahead of the vertical to maintain a free forward movement. When your horse is fully relaxed and going as he should, he will drop his head and round his back, and you will recognize the correct 'feel' of balance and rhythm. You will now be ready to progress to cavalletti.

Cavalletti are an essential piece of equipment for your training programme, and are quite easy to make. They are simply wooden rails with a crossed stand at each end (see diagram), which can be turned over and so used at three different heights. The rails should be thick so that a horse

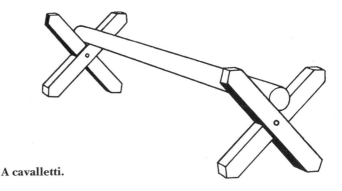

A cavalletti.

The trotting poles in front of these two small fences have put both pony and rider in perfect balance and rhythm to jump.

cannot displace them too easily, and hard so that they will not splinter.

Cavalletti can be used in the same way as trotting poles and you can vary the heights as you wish. It is a good idea to place several cavalletti around your schooling area at different heights: walking over them will teach the horse how to place himself and how to use his knees and hocks, and it will give the rider an exaggerated feel of his horse's back working under his weight. I am not too keen on trotting over the bigger cavalletti as the horse will tend to exaggerate his action and so lose his rhythm.

When you have established a good rhythm through four to six cavalletti, a small fence can be introduced 9-10 ft (2.74-3.05 m) away from the last pole or cavalletti, then another, one or two non-jumping strides away, and so on to form a lane, or 'chute', to use the American term. Make sure all your distances are accurate at this stage. You will probably have to establish the exact distances by trial and error to suit your particular animal. Later on you can vary your distances as a good exercise for shortening or lengthening your horse's stride, both trotting over poles and cantering between fences.

Riding in a circle over cavalletti must not be attempted until your horse has been properly schooled over cavalletti in a straight line. When working in a circle he must be bent to the inside, but at the same time his hind feet must follow exactly in the tracks of his front feet, otherwise he will become unbalanced. If a horse resists you when you try to bend him on his stiff side, he will try to throw his quarters out or drop his shoulders into the circle. The use of cavalletti in a circle will help to prevent this, as while he is stepping over the rails he will find it difficult to move on two tracks. Working in a circle over rails like this is a very good suppling exercise because, while the horse is bent to the inside, the outside neck and back muscles are stretched. It also enables you, by taking a larger or smaller circle, to vary the distance between the rails and so alter the horse's stride. It is, however, very hard work for the horse and extremely tiring, so you should never do it for too long at a time.

When you and your horse are working correctly with the cavalletti, you should be ready to graduate to small single fences. I say single fences, but to start with you should place a ground rail or cavalletti in front of each fence making sure you have a correct distance for one non-jumping stride. In this way your horse can trot to the cavalletti which he will quietly pop, and take one canter stride to the fence. Your ground rail should be just high enough to make him jump and not trot over it, so that he is correctly placed for the jump. In this way you ensure you can meet the fence on a correct stride and take off at exactly the right place without having to distract your horse by fiddling around and trying to find a stride. As a

beginner your horse will need all his concentration for the task in hand, jumping. These placing poles are invaluable in building confidence in both horse and rider and enable the rider to concentrate on his position without worrying about the correct approach. When your horse is jumping quietly and obediently with the placing pole you can progress to two small fences placed at a suitable distance apart. Later on you will vary the distance between the placing pole and the jump, or between two small fences placed first one, then two, then three strides apart, and this gymnastic work is a good exercise for developing your sense of stride.

All this work with cavalletti should be used in conjunction with your flat work. In this way you will not only make your horse supple and obedient, but the varied work will keep him keen, alert and interested in what he is doing. The same, I might say, applies to the rider. Very few young people enjoy endless hours of flat work. I used to hate it and still do. I am very lucky to be married to Brian, who trained with the Australian team under Franz Mairinger, one of the greatest trainers in the world. Franz himself spent several years instructing at the Spanish Riding School in Vienna before becoming the official trainer of the Australian teams. So Brian's sound knowledge of schooling on the flat is a product of this classical

background. Small wonder that when I get into difficulties I usually hand the horse over to him! Now, some of you may find the ground work very tedious, but when your schooling sessions include work with cavalletti and jumping lanes (chutes), they are infinitely more fun. In the same way an enjoyable ride out in the countryside will relax and freshen up both horse and rider after concentrated work in a confined area.

Later on the use of your jumping-lanes can be a great help should things start to go wrong. This is bound to happen sooner or later and even the most experienced horses lose confidence from time to time. You might make a bad mistake at a spread fence or a combination, or have a heavy fall, or it may be just an accumulation of small mistakes. Once a horse starts to lose confidence he will start 'backing' off' and so lose impulsion. This creates further problems as he will start to drop short on the back rail of spread fences, and he will not make enough ground on his combinations, and so frighten himself more. This must be corrected before he loses his nerve altogether, and here your jumping-lanes will prove invaluable. Keep the fences small and the distances accurate to start with, and as he gains confidence you can gradually make the distances longer to encourage him to lengthen his stride. A small but well-built spread fence at the end of your lane will help to restore his confidence over spreads. You can also use your jumping-lane to school a horse which is over-bold and careless, or inclined to rush his fences. These horses usually cover too much ground without getting the necessary height, jumping long and flat. If you keep the distances in your lane short, your horse will have to shorten his stride, bring his hocks under him and round his back over the fences. Jumping a short double of uprights is also a very good exercise for this.

There has always been great controversy about the subject of artificial schooling—rapping (known as 'poling' in the United States), jumping iron bars and using fences with a false ground line. No doubt these methods are still practised in certain stables although any such form of schooling is strictly forbidden at shows by the F.E.I., B.S.J.A., A.H.S.A., and the Australian federation. I have already said how important it is to build up your horse's confidence, and to resort to these methods is surely to destroy this confidence. To be able to jump well, particularly over today's big international courses, a horse must

A pleasant change. Both horse and rider can become bored with too much intensive schooling. It will do you both good to relax and get away from it all.

give himself time to use himself fully over every fence, and he must not be panicked into snatching his feet out of the way. In order to keep winning consistently at top level a horse must enjoy jumping and have confidence in both himself and his rider.

The psychological condition of your horse, how he feels, is always of the utmost importance, especially with a show jumper travelling hundreds of miles throughout the season. To perform consistently well, a horse has to be happy in what he is doing; a horse which is sour from overwork or too much jumping, or tired and stale from long travelling, will not jump well. So do not become so engrossed in your schooling that you don't give enough time to relaxation. Go out for a long ride and enjoy yourselves. In fact, you can further a young horse's education considerably by riding across country, up and down hills and over strange territory. He will learn to handle himself on different kinds of going and on uneven ground, and to adjust his pace, balance and stride accordingly. Walking up and down hills is, of course, a very good physical exercise: it will develop his muscles and his respiratory organs and strengthen his back, loins and hocks. Give him plenty of rein so that he can stretch his neck, use his shoulders and bring his hocks under him.

If you find a level patch of good ground, you can work the horse in a few circles, but do not concentrate on any one thing for too long at a time, as he will get bored. Pop him over any little logs, ditches or banks which you might come across so that he will accept jumping as part of his normal routine, but first always take a good look at the landing side first to make sure there are no holes, or bits of glass or wire.

These rides out in the country are enjoyable and your jumping lessons exciting, but you must continue with your schooling on the flat however reluctant you may be. You are aiming to get to the top and there is no short cut, no substitute for hard, dedicated work—believe me it will pay off in the end.

Your aim is to have complete control over a supple and obedient horse. Nothing less than this will succeed in show jumping today with courses as big and as technically demanding as they are. Before having full control over any horse, you must first be able to control his hind quarters, as it is from here that the power and propulsion are generated. To control the quarters, the rider must be

able to influence either hind leg with his own leg in complete co-ordination and rhythm with the horse. Thus, as the horse's off-hind leg leaves the ground to go forward, the rider's right lower leg should be in contact with the horse's side behind the saddle; as the near-hind moves forward, the left leg acts in the same way and so on, left right, left right. At the same time you use your weight through your seat bones, sitting deep into the saddle in rhythm with the horse. By influencing the quarters in this way, you will have the effect of pushing the hind leg forward under the centre of gravity, bringing about a free forward movement.

When you have your legs and weight working in rhythm with your horse, try and hold the bit in his mouth—this is putting your horse on the bit. The contact should be light and the horse should offer no resistance. He must accept the rider's leg, weight and hands as it is through these that the rider communicates with his horse.

Now you are ready to ask him to move away from your leg for a few steps and to start your work on two tracks or lateral movements. The aim of these movements is once again to improve balance, to supple the horse and keep him attentive and obedient. The aids for this work have been discussed in more detail in Chapter 3. These exercises should be practised only for a short time and your

Above and opposite: Jumping any little natural obstacles when out for a ride will add to your enjoyment while furthering your education.

horse should be allowed to move forward freely after each one. In all your work on two tracks, the forehand should remain in advance of the quarters. You must maintain impulsion at all times so that the pace remains regular and free. Nearly all horses are stiff on one side, usually the right, and you will find that this work on two tracks while concentrating more on his stiff side will help to make him more supple and obedient on both reins.

Always stop work before your horse becomes sour, remembering young horses will tire quickly when using muscles that are not fully developed. If you do too much work with him at any one time he may be stiff next day, and then he will start resisting you. If he should become upset or confused during a schooling session, walk him quietly away on a loose rein until he has calmed down. You will do nothing but harm if you carry on when the horse is in no state to understand what you are asking him to do. Always finish each lesson on a good note even if it means cutting it short or perhaps spending longer than you had intended. Some days he will go better than others and it is impossible to allot a set amount of time to any schooling session. When you are satisfied with his performance, reward him with a pat or a lump of sugar so that he knows he has done well. Loosen your girth and let him walk round on a loose rein to relax and cool off.

Adjusting your stride

5

Every successful athlete, equine or human, must be supple and fit, and therefore some gymnastic exercise is essential. As we have seen, cavalletti work supples and disciplines your horse and helps to establish rhythm, balance and co-ordination. Now you are ready to progress to more advanced exercises down the jumping-lanes (chutes) and over related distances, which will carry on the physical and mental education of both horse and rider.

At the risk of repeating myself, I would say again that

the most important attribute a top show jumper can have is a good eye. Some riders seem to possess an inborn sense of timing and stride but many more have to develop it through sheer hard work, concentration and practice. To jump clear rounds over international courses today, you have to be able to place your horse at the correct take-off place at each fence. A few brilliant horses can get themselves out of desperate trouble from time to time, but they cannot keep it up for long and will inevitably take to stopping sooner or later. You must be able to know exactly when and how to shorten or lengthen your horse's stride coming into a fence. You will find this work in varying related distances very good exercise for developing your eye.

You have already been using a ground rail in front of a fence as a placing pole, taking one normal non-jumping stride to a small jump. Now it is time to move the rail gradually closer to the fence and to shorten your horse's stride in the middle. When the distance is shorter your horse should not take off any nearer the fence but his stride should be shorter and more collected. You will do this by sitting deep into your saddle, closing your legs to push his hocks under him and keeping him well-balanced and collected in your hands.

Up to now you have been jumping with one stride between fences. The next stage is to make two, and then three, starting with a normal stride and then shortening the distance a little each time. The horse will soon gain confidence and learn to jump easily from a short stride.

Above: Jumping a short double. This horse is backing off, shortening his own stride instead of the rider doing the collecting. The rider is too far forward to push the hocks under, and she is resting her hands on the withers.

Right: Jumping the same double with the distance lengthened. Here the horse has jumped well into the double, but has flattened over the first fence. Although he is lengthening his stride, he has been allowed to go too much on his forehand with his hocks behind him, and so will also flatten over the second element.

Slipping a finger through the neck-strap will stop you being left behind and jabbing your horse in the mouth. The rider could give the pony a little more freedom over the fence—the neck-strap should be loose enough for you to take your hands forward with the movement of the horse so that he can drop his head and stretch his neck.

The rider is shortening the stride well, but the horse has resisted her hands and has brought his head too high. He will therefore have difficulty in rounding himself and folding his legs over the fence.

Here the approach is on a long stride; the rider is making the common mistake of 'pushing without keeping hold'. By losing contact with the horse's mouth she is letting him go on his forehand with the likelihood of flattening over the jump.

The next stage is to lengthen your stride. This is more difficult but basically the same rules apply. You must approach the first obstacle with more impulsion, and lengthen his stride while still keeping him balanced with his hocks under him, so that he does not pitch onto his forehand. Never lose contact with his mouth or stand up in your irons. As soon as you do this he will lose impulsion by pitching onto his forehand leaving his hocks behind him. You must lengthen his stride by pushing him forward with your weight (through your seat bones) and your legs while keeping hold of his head. One of the most common mistakes made by young novice riders is to let a horse go long and flat in the last two or three strides of the approach. He must drop his head coming into a fence, at the same time bringing his hocks further and further underneath him, so that his body is compressed into a spring; then he will have the necessary impulsion to jump the fence. This is just as important whether you are shortening or lengthening your stride.

With this basic training the horse will learn to accept the rider's influence in controlling his stride. Gradually you can move the fences further apart to give yourself three, four or more strides between them, and in this way you will learn to judge your stride from further back and to adjust it accordingly.

Throughout all these gymnastic exercises, I strongly advise the use of a neck strap. Even the best riders can get 'left behind' from time to time and the last thing a young,

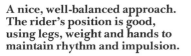

A nice, well-balanced approach. The rider's position is good, using legs, weight and hands to maintain rhythm and impulsion.

Opposite, top: The rider has lost contact with the horse's mouth by balancing her hands on his withers. She is pitched too far forward and will not be in control for at least two more strides.

Opposite, below: Here the rider has been left behind and in order to avoid interfering with the horse's head has allowed the reins to slip through her fingers. She must move her weight forward and collect the horse.

Below: A good position, although the rider's body has come back a fraction too soon. The weight should come down into the saddle as the hind legs come to the ground.

green horse needs in learning to jump is a jab in the teeth. Just hook one finger through the strap so that, if in trouble, you have something to hang onto other than the reins. A martingale strap is not a substitute, since pressure on it can affect a horse's head carriage.

Vary your fences using as many different kinds as possible, for instance a small wall, gate or brush, but do not jump anything big at this stage; there is absolutely no point in trying to see how high your horse or pony can jump. Time alone will tell you that. Most horses can jump the odd high single fence and to do so at this time will prove nothing. However, if he is jumping these small fences correctly, there is every chance that he will be able to perform as well over the bigger ones later on.

Varying the direction, distances and position of your fences will make your lessons more interesting and keep your horse attentive and alert. If you are working without an instructor, try and get someone to help you move the fences around and put up any fences you might knock down. It is very distracting for both you and your horse if you have to keep hopping off to adjust fences. It is also

The rider has stood up in his
irons (left) and is too far ahead of
his pony at this stage. As a result
he has lost contact (below)
through his legs and feet and his
knee is too far back on the saddle.
The landing position is quite
good (opposite) but the rider's
hands are too stiff. Although he
has not interfered with his
pony's mouth, he has lost
contact.

very useful to have someone on the ground to tell you when things are going wrong and why.

One fairly common problem arises with a horse who rushes his fences, usually a sign of apprehension. In this case, a line of four or five cavalletti in front of the fence, placed fairly close together, will make it impossible for him to rush as he will have to trot through the cavalletti. Similarly, some horses are inclined to dive off when they land, which two or three ground rails placed after the fence will discourage.

All your work with cavalletti, ground rails, distances and so on should be carried out with great care and patience. Always make sure the horse understands everything you ask of him and never push him beyond his capabilities. Remember, the longer you take, the quicker he'll make. Patience is all-important in any type of training and however well you finished up the day before, you must start the next day's lesson with an easy exercise. Never expect to carry on exactly where you left off and, as I said before, always try to finish on a good note, even if it means going back to something more basic.

Obstacles and courses

6

Basically there are four structural types of fences, of which all others are variations. These four basic types are the upright, the parallel, the staircase, and the pyramid. The structure of each fence dictates the most suitable place for the take-off and also the angle of descent on landing. This in turn affects the first few strides after a fence so that with a line of related fences, particularly combinations, the structure of the fences has a tremendous bearing on the stride measurements between them.

The course for an international show at Lucerne.

Most riders have their own methods of measuring distances; while generally you should not be afraid of asking advice, you should *never* rely on asking another rider how a certain distance measures. Always walk it yourself. I personally always measure from what should be the highest point of the horse's parabola over each jump. For example, with an upright to a parallel I measure from the upright to the middle of the parallel, with a parallel to a staircase from the middle of the parallel to the highest point of the staircase.

Allowances should be made for the solidity of the fence, bearing in mind that you can ride more strongly into a well-built solid fence than a fiimsy one.

Several other factors must be taken into consideration, like the state of the ground and any slope; soft ground and an uphill slope will shorten a horse's stride while firm ground and a downhill slope will lengthen it. These are all things that you will learn only from experience, but a study of distance measurements in relation to fence structure will at least give you a basic guide to work on.

Let's have a look at the different sorts of fence in turn. An upright fence is one whose elements are in the same vertical plane. If it has a ground line in front of it it ceases to be a true upright. An oxer or parallel is a spread fence; a true parallel is one in which the two highest elements are of the same height. This is the most difficult fence to jump and demands great accuracy. If the front element is lower than the back one, or again if there is a ground line on the take-off side, it is no longer a true parallel and becomes

This type of upright fence must be jumped from a collected stride. The series of poles in a vertical plane tends to emphasise the height of a fence, whereas more filling at the base gives a more definite ground line and makes it easier to jump.

A true parallel, or oxer. In order to clear both elements of such a fence the highest point of the horse's jump must be over the centre of the fence.

A staircase fence, or triple bar, with plenty of filling to make it an easy fence to jump. It requires a bold approach with the take-off close to the front element.

easier to jump. the staircase fence usually has three elements in a sloping plane with the back rail the highest point. A triple bar is a true staircase fence but there are many variations which can be either very easy or very difficult to jump. It can be an open triple bar, with just three poles, or one filled in with brush fences or walls. The slopes can be steep or flat, convex or concave; or the middle element can be omitted, as in an open ditch or small water with a pole behind. The pyramid fence is the old type of hog's back jump with the highest element in the centre; this is the easiest fence to jump for as long as you come in sufficiently close to the take-off for your horse to clear the middle part, the far element is unimportant. A water-jump comes under the category of a pyramid fence, as the horse should come close to the take-off side and the highest part of his jump should be over the centre of the water.

Bouncer jumping in a Nations'
Cup in 1964. Here is a variation
of the staircase fence with less
solid filling than the one shown
opposite. Over this type of fence
the highest point of the horse's
jump must be over the third
element.

The water jump comes into the
category of a pyramid fence.
The highest point of the horse's
jump should be over the centre
of the water.

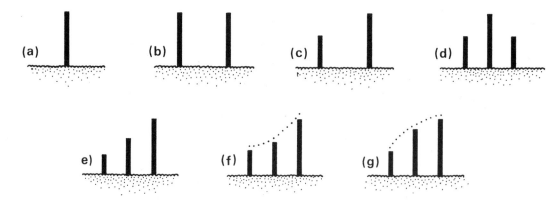

Types of obstacle: (a) vertical, (b) square parallel, (c) sloping parallel, (d) pyramid fence, (e) staircase, (f) concave staircase, (g) convex staircase.

Jumping a low parallel.

The most suitable place for take-off varies in distanc from each fence according to its size and structure; wit the staircase and pyramid types of fence it is obviousl advisable to come in close when the take-off rail is low; th ideal distance to take-off from an upright will var according to your horse's scope and athletic ability. rough guide for an upright of up to about 4 ft 6 in (1.3 m) is to take off from the height of the fence away, but u to this height a horse with plenty of liberty can easily stan off a lot further away, and an athletic one can come i closer. Above this height the take-off point will get close as the fence becomes higher. When jumping a 7 ft (2.1 m) puissance wall, a horse has to take off very close i order to clear the great height. The distance of take-o from a parallel will very according to whether or not it sloping and how much. There's very little margin of erro

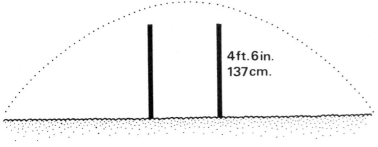

4ft.6in.
137cm.

As the obstacle height increases beyond about 4 ft 6 in (137 cm) the take-off point will become closer and the angle of descent steeper in relation to the height of the fence.

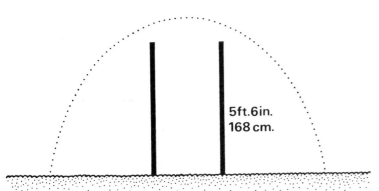

5ft.6in.
168 cm.

Below: When landing over a big fence a horse is inclined to pitch onto his forehand, so losing his pace and rhythm. Here, although Sportsman is landing at a very steep angle, David Broome has maintained balance and the horse will continue and carry on without loss of impulsion.

with a true parallel as in order to clear the height of both elements of the spread the highest point of a horse's jump must be over the centre of the oxer. Jumping a low wide oxer is a very good exercise for a young horse as it will make him drop his head, round his back and form a good bascule. However, as it demands such great accuracy it is advisable to use a placing pole to ensure a correct take-off.

Thus the structure of the fence determines the parabola of a horse's jump and therefore the angle of his descent. If his angle is gradual then he can move away from the fence smoothly and easily, but if it is steep he will pitch more onto his forehand. This is why you must take into consideration the type of fences involved when measuring the distance between them. A horse will obviously cover less ground over a big wide parallel than he will over a flat triple bar or a small upright. When a horse pitches after a steep descent his first stride is cramped and he loses pace and rhythm, so extra impulsion is required to cope with this problem. The normal canter stride of an average horse is 12 ft (3.66 m). A simple but very rough guide when measuring, as I do, from the highest point of the horse's jump, is that fences placed at multiples of 12 ft (3.66 m) apart are at approximately the correct distance.

Debbie Johnsey jumping water as a junior.

Jumping a water jump should, in theory, present no problem to a horse—after all, his normal stride is 12 ft (3.66 m) and even an Olympic water is only 16 ft (4.9 m) wide. Unfortunately however it seldom works out so easily and the fault usually lies with the rider. Most novice horses start jumping water well, as they tend to spook at it and jump high. (A horse which stops at water or will not go near it is another problem, and you will need a lot of patient schooling over very small waters to win his confidence.) If he gains enough height he will have no difficulty in jumping the width. It is a common mistake for riders to gallop flat out at the water. The horse then reaches it long and flat with his hocks out behind him, usually jumping straight into it. Once a horse starts to jump into water he quickly loses his respect for it and jumps low and flat, landing in the water or on the tape every time. This is very difficult to correct, but placing a pole over the water will help to get him into the air again. A balanced, collected approach full of impulsion, with the take-off close to the near-side, is ideal.

A young horse should be given an early introduction to permanent fences such as water-jumps, hedges, banks, and ditches. The ideal is to build some small natural fences at home. Permanent show-grounds which feature these natural obstacles have long been a part of the European show circuit but only gradually, over the last fifteen or so years since the innovation of Hickstead, have they become established in Britain, and even more recently in the US. There are still very few, if any, in Australia. Many novice horses now have plenty of opportunity to become familiar with these courses in miniature during their early competitive lives, before being confronted with them at international level. Even so, the show-ring is not the best place to introduce the horse to an entirely strange obstacle, however small, and it is advisable to do some schooling over them at home if possible.

To start with, your water and dry ditches should be small enough for a horse to trot over them; 3-4 ft (91-122 cm) wide is plenty big enough. He must learn to tackle them with confidence, but also with respect, so they should be made deep enough to teach him that he should not put his feet down in them. When he is jumping quietly over these you can progress to something a little bigger, but take great care not to frighten him at this stage.

Of course, it is out of the question to build a fence like the Derby bank at home, but by the time your horse has reached the standard required to jump this type of obstacle, he should have the experience and confidence to tackle anything he is asked. The golden rule to remember when coming down a steep bank, like the ones at Hickstead and Hamburg, is to keep your horse absolutely straight, and balanced between hands and legs. It is when the hind legs start to slip sideways that a fall usually occurs. The idea is to keep hold of his head, while still allowing him enough rein to use his head and neck to balance himself, and to keep your weight over his centre of gravity; do not lean back.

I well remember the first time the Derby bank appeared in a competition at Hickstead. Douglas Bunn had decided to introduce the bank to horses and riders at the meeting before the very first Derby there was due to take place. In the Derby itself, horses jump onto the bank over a small post and rail fence, and then run up a gradual slope to the top where there is another small fence, followed by the nearly sheer drop at the far end. At the bottom there is a large upright fence just two strides away. In the Derby Trial, which is now held at the same meeting usually two days before the Derby, horses are given an opportunity to negotiate the bank by turning left at the top and coming down the more gradual side. At this meeting before the first Derby in 1961, Douglas decided to give the riders a rehearsal of the real thing by allowing us to come down this gradual side. When we walked the course, we climbed up onto the bank, stood at the top of the 10 ft 6 in (3.2 m) descent and looked down. I think 'horror' is the word which best describes our feelings at that moment. I have lost count of the number of times I have come down the bank since then, yet every year I still experience a slight sense of shock each time I stand on the edge of that sheer drop. What is more, while most fences look more inviting from on top of a horse, the bank looks far worse as you are about another 10 ft (3.05 m) higher up.

As is usually the case, the riders' concern at that time was mainly for their horses. This was certainly not a show jump, and bore no resemblance to anything we had seen in a show-ring. Furthermore, while we were quite prepared to take a calculated risk with our valuable horses over the ditches, waters and small banks, this seemed to border on recklessness! An argument started which soon developed into a big row, with several of the leading riders threatening to withdraw their horses. I was as dubious as any about the bank, but Brian, having successfully negotiated several steep slides in three-day events, assured me that it was nowhere near as hazardous as it looked. As we had only been married about three weeks, I didn't feel inclined to argue with him! After much heated discussion, Douglas agreed to put another fence—a 5 ft 7 in (1.7 m) gate—alongside the bank, thus giving the riders an alternative. In fact, most of the riders came down the bank, and although one unfortunate injury was caused by a rider sitting back and keeping too strong a hold on his horse's head, there was very little trouble.

The first ever British Jumping Derby was held a few weeks later, and there was no serious trouble at the bank, with faults coming all round the course, as happens every year. That great Irish rider, Seamus Hayes, jumped the only clear round to win, and I was one of the lucky ones who tied second with four faults on Thou Swell. Annoyingly I was the only rider to have one of the easiest fences on the course down, the rail going off the 'road fence'.

Coming down the Derby Bank.

The steep side of the bank which is used in the Derby has admittedly caused a few problems and accidents over the years, and since those early days, while the rest of the course has undoubtedly become much bigger, the descent of the bank itself has been slightly modified. The Hickstead bank is still higher and steeper than its Hamburg counterpart; it is in fact the largest in the world, but as long as a horse comes down straight and balanced, he should find no problems. The bank has now become an accepted risk among most of the world's leading riders. Certainly the element of danger gives the Derby tremendous spectator appeal, and brings people flocking in their thousands to watch one of the greatest show-jumping events in the world.

I have given some information at the end of this book about the various competitions open to horses of each grade, and I have recommended those I think suitable for horses graduating from novice to more advanced level. There are of course maximum height restrictions on fences in all novice and junior classes run under the rules of most national federations, and these you will find in the yearly rule book. Apart from this, the type of courses you are likely to meet will depend entirely on the standard of the show, the course-builder, and the fence material at his disposal.

Permanent show grounds which feature the natural cross-country type of fence will, I believe, provide the setting for show jumping in the future. With their endless variety, these courses are far more interesting to ride and they certainly have more spectator appeal.

Through the winter months, of course, the indoor shows are now a firmly established part of the show-jumping calendar. With these now becoming more and more popular you may well be starting your jumping career in the small indoor schooling shows; these usually have a 'clear-round class' in which there is no jump-off, and ribbons are given for clear rounds. This is ideal for the novice horse and rider because very often you are allowed to jump round more than once if you wish.

Riding indoors is not so very different from riding outside. The same principles apply, but it is even more important to make full use of what little room you have and to maintain impulsion at all times, particularly round the corners. It is a risky practice to come round a corner waiting for a stride as you have so little time to ride for one when you find it. Keep your eye on the next fence all the way round the turn and try to find your stride as you come, without losing impulsion.

In a small indoor arena like Wembley, in London, there are very often two or three fences placed next to each other, and a horse may come round the corner and set his sights on the wrong fence. The rider then has to check him back and readjust his stride to the correct fence, by which time it is probably too late. You must hold him together and guide him with your legs and hands around the track you intend to take, always concentrating on the *next* fence, so that you have his attention all the time.

David Broome, riding Philco, in Amsterdam, demonstrates the art of riding indoors. About to jump a fence coming out of a turn in a speed class he has turned the corner full of impulsion with the horse perfectly balanced between his hands and legs. Note the look of concentration on the face of both horse and rider.

From ponies to horses

7

The transition from ponies to horses is probably the most crucial stage of your show-jumping career. In the UK a junior rider is now allowed to ride horses in senior classes from the year of his fourteenth birthday, while still being eligible to ride ponies in junior classes. This enables him to make the change over a gradual period. Junior riders in the UK have a tremendous advantage over their rivals on the Continent, as the British native pony breeds give them a wide selection of animals to choose from. They can therefore start their riding and jumping on ponies, while many of the junior riders on the Continent of Europe have to compete on horses right from the beginning. It is much easier for a child to learn to handle a pony of the right size than a big horse on which his legs barely reach the girth. On the Continent it is quite usual to see a tiny child learning to ride on a sixteen-hand horse, and looking like a pea on a drum. Nevertheless I think most juniors in Britain stay on ponies too long —many children of thirteen or fourteen are far too big for a 14.2 pony anyway—and then they find even greater difficulty in riding horses.

I'm quite sure that you should graduate to horses as soon as you are big enough and strong enough, if at all possible. In Britain there are many young riders' classes at shows up and down the country which are an ideal stepping-stone from junior to senior competitions. On the other hand, not very many American junior riders begin their equestrian careers on ponies. It's a shame, since too many youngsters are overmounted on horses far too large for them, and these people never have the feeling of riding a proportionally right animal.

My advice to you in the first chapter of this book was to start your career on an old pony who knows his job. I think the same applies, but possibly to a lesser extent, when you come out of juniors. An experienced horse, not necessarily a brilliant one, but one who knows his job, will probably teach you a lot more than a novice. Furthermore, you may find that a novice horse-and-rider combination will run into trouble, and you will teach each other bad habits. However, it is never easy to find a good experienced horse to carry a young rider; the demand vastly exceeds the supply, and a bad horse, an unsound one or a 'stopper' will do you more harm than good. If you are to ride a complete novice, it is even more vital for you to have help and instruction, and indeed advice on selecting the horse. Remember the horse with a future is not necessarily the one which wins the most novice competitions, in fact very often the reverse. Over small courses, the short-striding ultra-careful horses without much scope are usually very hard to beat, but these very rarely reach beyond novice level. What is more, they are clever at putting in short strides and making their own arrangements, and you will learn nothing but bad habits from them.

Without going into detail about correct conformation

Debbie Johnsey, now a successful senior, jumping in her junior days on the pony stallion Champ V.

here (show jumpers come in all shapes and sizes!) the most important assets in a young horse are a perfect temperament, natural balance and a good action.

A successful jumper must be bold, courageous, honest and mentally stable and yet he must have that little extra personality and individuality which makes a top performer—star quality, if you like. His balance is determined largely by his conformation and although this can be improved with schooling, a naturally well-balanced horse will obviously have a tremendous advantage.

Action is very important; this again depends a great deal on conformation. I like to see a good knee-action in a jumper. He must pick his feet up and bend his knees over a fence, so it is obviously a good sign if he does this when moving naturally. The two best jumpers I have ever ridden, Spring Fever and Bouncer, both have very exaggerated knee-action. At the walk, he should move straight and clean off the ground, picking his feet up high and putting them down square; when trotting, he should move freely, bending his knees and hocks, using his shoulder and following through behind. The length of a horse's stride is more important in a jumper than his size; a small horse can have a long stride and this makes him ride like a big one. Stroller was one very good example of this. Some really big horses have stuffy, short strides and they ride like ponies; a short-striding horse is usually more active and easier to ride, particularly indoors. However, a long stride is an advantage over a big, spready course and with long distances in combinations.

Control of stride being of the utmost importance, the ideal is to have a horse with a fairly long stride who will shorten it and 'bounce' at the command of his rider. Tony Newbery's great little Australian horse, Warwick, is a deceptive small horse; Tony always rides him on a short bouncy stride but he has tremendous acceleration, and can lengthen his stride from almost a standstill to the normal stride of a big horse in a combination.

Of course, when choosing a young novice horse, it is impossible to tell whether it will ever reach beyond the novice level. Nevertheless you can get some idea of his potential when you see him jump. His approach to a fence should be bold but unhurried; he should come in quietly with his ears pricked and looking where he's going. When in the air he should drop his head, really use his neck and back and round himself over the fence. If he happens to

Debbie Johnsey again, shown this time as an adult rider, on her Olympic horse Moxy in an international competition at Lucerne.

The special feeling of jumping in an indoor competition at Wembley.

hit a fence, it is interesting to see how he will jump it the next time. If he backs off, it is not a bad thing because it shows he didn't like hitting it. He should really fold his legs away and jump big this time. If on the other hand he comes down and clouts it again, you had better think twice about buying him! Your show jumper must be bold and brave, but he must also dislike hitting fences, an unfortunately rare combination. This is why top show jumpers are so hard to find.

There are literally thousands of young horses brought out every year all over the world—how many of them leave the ranks of novices, let alone reach international level? A very, very small proportion. Of course as you progress through and out of junior classes you will not necessarily be looking for an Olympic horse! Nevertheless, you will probably have a long search ahead of you before you find a good, genuine, honest, sound horse that will suit your purpose. But do not be impatient and settle for anything less, for once you have the right tool to work with, your task will be that much easier and the odds against you reaching your ultimate goal a little shorter.

Summer Madness, Spring Fever's first foal, at his very first show. This is a typical example of a novice horse jumping too extravagantly through inexperience. Although he is rounding his back well, he has not yet learned to fold his legs.

76

Planning your season

8

In every training programme the key to success is to plan ahead. Just as it is important in your early schooling at home to plan your lessons well in advance, your programme of shows should be mapped out several weeks ahead. Of course, this schedule will be subject to change as will your schooling programme. A lot will depend on how well you and your horse are performing and there are several other factors which may contribute—the fitness and well-being of your horse, the weather conditions, the state of the ground, the type of courses you meet and the classes available to you, and even the state of your finances. But you must have some sort of programme devised. You may be a novice rider with an experienced horse, or you may both be beginners. Either way, it is advisable to start off at the small unaffiliated shows. In Britain now there are a number of these shows which are not affiliated to the British Show Jumping Association.

The B.S.J.A. is the British national federation. In the United States the national federation is the A.H.S.A. (American Horse Shows Association) and in Australia it is the E.F.A. (Equestrian Federation of Australia). Most other countries where show jumping is an established sport have similar bodies to organize it. The F.E.I. (Federation Equestre Internationale) is the international federation under whose rules all international shows are held. Most shows in Britain which are not affiliated to the B.S.J.A. are nevertheless run under B.S.J.A. rules with standard fences and a recognized course-builder, and therefore provide an excellent kindergarten for the young horse and rider who want to gain experience. The standard of jumping is usually lower, and the courses smaller than at the affiliated shows.

Through the winter months, when there are fewer big shows, these unaffiliated shows are mostly indoors and they are an ideal preparation for the season ahead. With the standard of show jumping and the number of new recruits increasing each year, even the classes for the complete novice at affiliated shows, i.e. 'Foxhunter', 'Junior Foxhunter' or 'Newcomers', demand a horse or pony with some competitive experience. The great advantage of these unaffiliated shows is that they provide the necessary experience, without the undesirable possibility of your horse winning prize money towards upgrading. Perhaps I should explain here that a horse is graded according to the amount of prize money he has won, and the grading determines what classes he may jump in at shows. This system applies with some variations of detail in all the main show-jumping countries.

In the summer, too, there are numerous unaffiliated shows throughout Britain, and some affiliated shows have unaffiliated jumping in their second or third rings.

Americans too run schooling shows to introduce their green horses to competition. These are informal, local events which feature classes such as 'Novice Hunter', or

Jumping a parallel at a county show.

'Pre-Green Hunter'. The courses are relatively short and quite inviting, and even horses and ponies that are not strictly 'hunter' type enter. Then they progress into the Jumper Division, also at schooling shows, before graduating to more advanced levels, such as Preliminary Jumper, Intermediate Jumper, and finally (based on age, experience, and winnings) Open Jumper. Although schooling shows are seldom recognized by the American Horse Shows Association, these more advanced classes are conducted at recognized shows, and so membership in the A.H.S.A. is virtually a prerequisite for exhibiting jumpers or competing as a rider.

Although you will want to start with small courses, try to pick the shows with a good set of fences and a course builder who knows his job. If it is the indoor season, try to avoid the small, poky arenas which will inevitably involve

When exercizing on a show-ground you should be correctly turned out and wear protective head-covering.

several twists and turns in the course—not a good idea for a novice horse or rider. If outdoors, the ground is important. Obviously, it is neither desirable to have rock-hard going nor to be knee-deep in mud. Of course, there will often be no way of knowing these things until you arrive at the show. But it is never too late to change your mind if you are not happy about the course or the ground. Nobody ever did any harm by not jumping and even if you have hired a horse-box or trailer to take you to the show and Granny and Grandad and your parents and brothers and sisters have all come to watch you, be strong-minded enough to say there is always another day. You can do untold damage to a young horse if you frighten him with a false distance or jar him up on hard ground, and he may never forget it.

The same applies to jumping against the clock. It is very

I have heard of non-interference but this is ridiculous! Ferdi Tyteca jumping Exakt over the wall at Wembley. This is certainly not a practice to be recommended.

81

tempting to 'have a cut' when your friends and relatives are all cheering you on, but nothing ruins a young horse quicker than jumping fast. He will lose his balance, his rhythm, his jump and finally his confidence and you will undo everything you have worked so hard to achieve. What is more, this chasing against the clock can do as much harm to your riding as to your horse. Only very experienced riders can maintain precision at speed and you will very soon lose your accuracy if you attempt it so early in your career. Lately, when taking my own two children to the small shows with their ponies, I have watched with horror very young children riding their ponies flat-out against the clock with their parents in the collecting ring actually shouting encouragement! (This is a greater problem in Britain than America—few American shows hold time classes for junior riders, and those which do restrict them to experienced horses and horsemen.)

This is certainly not the fault of the child and probably most of the parents do not know any better. Very often the blame lies with the course-builder, firstly for building the fences too small in the first place—it is far more dangerous to jump small fences at a flat-out gallop than to jump bigger fences slowly; and secondly for designing the jump-off course with too much room between fences. A shorter, twistier track would encourage riders to go more steadily and take the shortest route. In this way they would *have* to have their ponies balanced and under control in order to execute the sharp turns, but unfortunately, at most of these junior shows anyway, it is a mad gallop with reins and legs flapping which usually ends up the winning round.

Certainly this is not show jumping and bears no resemblance to it. What is more, while most ponies seem to have six legs and the agility of a cat, you will be hard put to find a horse with such athletic ability. This is largely why junior riders find the transition from ponies to horses so difficult. Any child can sit on a good pony, do absolutely nothing and look brilliant, but horses take a lot more riding. How often one sees a top-class junior fade from the limelight after he or she has graduated from junior classes.

It takes a very strong-minded and dedicated child to resist the temptation to try and win, particularly if the child has the competitive spirit which is so essential in top-class jumping. Without the will to win you will never succeed. But remember, these early, novice classes are only a stepping-stone to the real thing and your turn will come, if you think and plan ahead to your ultimate goal.

This will not be easy. Even the top riders never tire of winning rosettes or ribbons, if only a minor award down the line. They will probably put it in a box at home with all the others and never look at it again, but at least for an hour or two that ribbon is proof of something well done. So it is especially hard for a young rider who is new to the game to keep jumping clear rounds and yet always finish up out of the money. But, remember, you are aiming for bigger things—so don't let your supporters persuade you to 'have a go' just this once. Leave these small fish to riders who have no ambition to go any further and wait for the bigger fry.

The thrill of winning. Eddie Macken on Boomerang receives the trophy for the British Jumping Derby at Hickstead in 1976. Throughout the 1976 season this combination performed with brilliant consistency at all the important international shows.

On the day

9

I have already stressed the importance of planning ahead, not only in your training programme but in selecting your shows and classes through the season. Unfortunately, entries have to be made well in advance of the date of the show and your choice of classes will obviously depend on how you and your horse are going. Your rate of progress will be varied and there are bound to be setbacks so it is advisable to leave yourself with a choice of classes if possible. This can become rather expensive but will prove a sound investment in the long run.

No matter how well your horse is going it will do him good to drop back to a lower grade from time to time for a let-down. This is particularly true of a young horse and for this reason it is wise to start jumping him in a higher grade of class while he is still eligible to compete in the lower one. If once he is up-graded things should go wrong and he should lose confidence, you can always get permission to jump *hors concours* in a smaller class even if he is no longer eligible.

If you can pick out a few three- or four-day shows, where you can stable, you will find that both you and your horse will benefit enormously. You may well find that you have the choice of two or three classes each day, possibly in different rings, each with a strange set of fences and a different course-builder. In this way you will gain more experience in these few days than you will in half-a-dozen weekend shows. Staying away from home will prove a good education for both of you. Your horse will get used to the atmosphere and activity of a big show and learn to accept it as his normal routine. It will give you a perfect opportunity to learn by watching and listening to other riders. If you keep your eyes and ears open you will pick up several useful bits of information—and some useless, no doubt!—not only about show jumping but about horsemanship in general, stable management, veterinary care, etc.

Whether you are staying at a show or just going away for one day, always allow yourself plenty of time before your class is scheduled to start. Find out if they are running to time and when you have to walk the course. Have a look at the warming-up area and the practice fences and pay particular attention to the going both outside and in the ring; see whether you have to jump in a drawn order or whether you have to put your number down with the collecting ring steward. If this is the case, then it is a good idea to jump fairly late in the order so that you can watch a few rounds jumped and see how the course rides. Very often there is one particular fence which is causing trouble. Perhaps it is on an angle or out of a tight turn; maybe there is a shadow across it or it is on unlevel ground; it may be just a difficult fence to jump. There could be any number of reasons—you will learn a lot by watching the other riders. This is particularly important

Above: A good pair of lined leather brushing boots with extra protection on the inside. The over-reach boots (bell boots) are to protect the heels against over-reaching by the hind shoes, most likely to happen in very deep ground.

Opposite: Any young horse must become used to the general activities of the show ground. Here are the stabling arrangements at Hickstead.

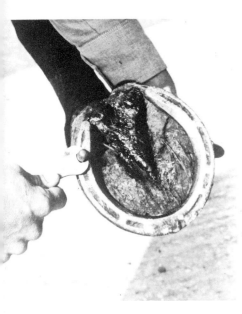

Inserting a stud in the outside quarter of a shoe.

when you are jumping indoors as there are usually several related distances between fences due to the restricted area.

Allow yourself plenty of time before the class starts to tack your horse up, put his boots on and studs in, and so on before you start to warm him up. I strongly advise the use of brushing boots when jumping, because even the straightest mover will strike into himself once in a while. These boots should be well made and fit snugly to give maximum protection, but never put them on too tight. If you have a long wait between classes, or before a jump-off, loosen the straps, or take the boots off to give the legs a rest. Over-reach boots (bell boots) are necessary on some horses who are inclined to over-reach, that is, to strike into the front heels with the hind feet. Bandages can be used for support when jumping either on hard ground or very deep going, but again these should never be left on for any length of time. When bandaging, make sure that you have an even pressure all the way down to the fetlock joint; this is where the support is most needed. However, bandages incorrectly applied can do more harm than good and they do not give nearly as much protection against a horse hitting himself as a well-made, lined leather boot.

Studs have long been considered an essential part of a show jumper's equipment in Britain and are fast becoming so in the United States and Australia. Long before the start of your class you should have decided which studs to use, depending on the type of going. If the ground is hard you will need small, sharp studs all round, and if it is deep, then you need large, square ones. With good ground I always use small studs in front and bigger ones behind, putting one stud in the outside quarter of each shoe. Some people prefer to put two studs in each foot, one at each heel, but here there is a danger that a horse will tread on himself with the inside stud. Unless the show ground is entirely free from hard surfaces it is best to put your studs in when you reach the practice area or collecting ring. This will save your horse the uncomfortable experience of having to walk on a hard surface with 'high heels'.

Having tacked your horse up and checked that everything is fitted correctly, you are ready to start your warming-up period. With a young horse it is a good idea to spend the first ten minutes or so just walking him around, so that he will settle down and relax before you ask him to do any work. Some horses need more warming up than

There is generally a certain amount of tension in the atmosphere before a big class. In the inside collecting room at Wembley horses are waiting their turn to jump, and officials make sure competitors are on time to jump in the correct order.

others, the aim being to get them supple, responsive and obedient. There is no need to work him into the ground before a class and as soon as he is relaxed and supple on the flat, and you have his concentration, then you can give him a few small jumps over a practice fence. Here again the idea is to get his mind on the job and his muscles tuned up so that he is really using himself properly. In my opinion, it is completely unnecessary and pointless to jump anything big in the collecting ring before any competition, particularly a novice one. Your aim is to get your horse jumping confidently and quietly and you will achieve nothing by having your competition outside the ring.

While on the subject of working a horse on the show ground and jumping in the collecting ring I must stress the importance of good behaviour at shows. Remember, the other competitors have as much right to the facilities as you have, and courtesy and consideration for others are as important on a show ground as on a public highway. This is particularly so in the collecting ring, as these are very often small and overcrowded.

When jumping a practice fence, make quite sure that the way is clear, and that there is nobody about to cross your path. If somebody else is there before you, wait your

Junior riders walk the course at Wembley before their competition. Notice the general discussion at the obstacles among young competitors, their parents and trainers. The picture gives an idea of how tight the courses can be indoors.

turn; and if you want the fence raised or lowered, wait until the riders in front of you have finished jumping it. You should have allowed yourself enough time to be able to suffer these delays without panic. When you are working on the flat keep as far away from the practice fence as you can. If you have to cross behind a fence or in front of one, either on a horse or on foot, always look carefully each way as if crossing a road. These areas can often be extremely dangerous, and I have seen several nasty accidents occur, either through impatience, lack of courtesy, or sheer carelessness. I am glad to say that over the last few years the F.E.I. and the B.S.J.A. have introduced some long-overdue rules about the correct use of practice fences. Where possible, there must be one upright and one spread obstacle in the practice area. These must be correctly built, and flagged to be jumped in one direction only. These rules are now strictly enforced for the safety of all concerned. Courtesy and consideration are important elsewhere on the show ground too. Remember, many of the officials are acting in an honorary capacity, and they are usually doing their best to help the competitors. If the show secretary has made a mistake with your entries be patient and keep calm; give him/her time to sort it out.

The stewards in the collecting ring also have a very hard job trying to ensure that the competitors are ready to jump in their correct order, so try and help them by being ready when they call you. The riders' co-operation with the stewards and officials will always help the show to run smoothly and efficiently.

The course-builder has an unenviable task as it is impossible to please all the competitors all the time. You have to take the rough with the smooth, but if there is anything in the course you think might harm your horse, particularly if he's a novice, you can always withdraw quietly. Even the best course-builders sometimes make mistakes, and when the experienced riders consider there is a genuine error, such as a false distance, then they can appeal to the judges.

The judges, too, have a pretty thankless task, so treat them with respect, and remember that their word is final. If you are jumping in a valuable competition and you feel that a genuine mistake has been made in the judging, you may lodge an official objection with the appropriate deposit according to the rules under which the class is being judged. But *never* try to argue personally with a judge. Unless there is a lot of money or prestige at stake it is usually better to suffer the injustice without making a fuss.

Finally, a word about dress. It is a mark of respect to turn both yourself and your horse out well. All competitors must wear correct hunting clothes, with collars and ties or stocks, and protective head-covering must be worn both in the ring and when jumping a practice fence.

If you are reprimanded for any breach of discipline or misconduct keep calm and apologise, even if you feel you are the victim of an injustice. It does you no good to lose your temper, and it is easy to get upset over even the smallest thing if you happen to be suffering from nerves.

Most competitors feel a bit tense before a big competition. This is not necessarily a bad thing. We all suffer from ring nerves from time to time, but as many a great actor will tell you, being nervous can very definitely improve your performance. It can also destroy it completely, so if you suffer excessively from nerves, you must try to get the better of them if you possibly can. It is entirely natural to feel tense and keyed up before you go into the ring, but as long as you keep your head you will find that, with the adrenalin flowing, your reflexes will be more alert, your reactions quicker, and your performance will be just that little bit more polished and efficient.

Before a class begins, you will walk the course. If you are drawn early in the order of going, you will probably warm up before doing so. Before walking the course for any competition you should study the plan of the course, which will be displayed in or near the collecting ring. Some course plans have a continuous line showing the track you must take; study this carefully, as any deviation from this track—going the wrong side of a flag, for example—entails elimination. Make sure you know where the start and finish are and check on the table under which the class is judged, the speed required and the time allowed (if a factor). By watching the first few horses go—and keeping an eye on the public clock if there is one—you will be able to see whether the course distance has been measured short, as sometimes happens, or whether you have plenty of time.

If you are now advanced enough to enter a speed class, try to work out the shortest route. Remember, the fastest time is put up by the riders who take the shortest line and not by those who gallop flat out. There are bound to be fences you can take on an angle and places where you can cut corners, and if you have studied the plan beforehand you will have more time to concentrate on your course when you walk it.

When jumping against the clock, it is important to study the line that you intend to take over the whole course. You can save time in the air by jumping across a fence at an angle so that you land in the direction of the next fence. It's extraordinary how a good horse can jump a really big fence out of a sharp turn from only one or two strides away, but he *must* be perfectly balanced and have plenty of impulsion. On the turn you must sit deep into your saddle with your outside seat bone, your outside leg controlling the amount of turn, and your weight possibly even a little behind the vertical.

It is usually easy to jump a fence on a turn, as there is room to adjust your approach by taking a shorter line or by going wider. It is also easy for the horse taking this line, as the inside shoulder is free, and the inside hind leg is coming under the centre of gravity. However, if you go *past* the centre line of the fence, the horse has to turn back towards the fence, so his inside shoulder is cramped, and you leave yourself no room to adjust his stride.

You should always take into account the position of the next fence as this will influence the way you jump the one

You must pace the distance between related fences to see whether you will need to shorten or lengthen your stride. If the distance is more than 72 ft (22 m) it is not necessary as you will have plenty of room to adjust your stride. Be sure you know how long your own stride is!

before. Valuable seconds can also be saved by taking the shortest line through the start to the first fence, and from the last fence to the finish. Make a mental note of all these things when you walk your course.

Never underestimate the importance of walking the course! Very often you will see riders walking around deep in conversation or enjoying a joke amongst themselves and not bothering to study the fences or pace the distances. Now obviously the top riders are experienced enough not to have to worry too much about walking a novice course (you will seldom see them playing the fool when there is a big prize at stake!), but you will need to study every detail in order to give yourself and your horse the best chance. Remember your horse has no way of knowing what particular problems await him, so you must study not only the individual fences but the course as a whole. You should walk the line that you intend to take between fences, particularly with a young horse so that you can give him as much room as possible to maintain free forward movement. Make full use of your arena, especially indoors, and try to avoid tight turns which will unbalance and distract him. If you think there is any particular fence which he might dislike (and you should have discovered your horse's likes and dislikes before you get to the show), be prepared and give him every assistance to jump it and no opportunity to stop or duck out. This is easier said than done!

If you think he might spook at any particular fence, ride past it when you enter the ring, but take care not to get eliminated for 'showing an obstacle' to your horse!

Always make full use of the short time you are allowed in the ring before the signal goes for you to start your round. Most young riders just wander their horses into the ring and walk or jog them around in a small circle waiting for the signal to go, and then canter straight through the start. Try and get into the ring as soon as you can, and collect your horse and pull him together to show him this is serious. Give him a good sharp canter around the ring so that he has a chance to look at his surroundings; this is especially important with a young horse as he will be very easily distracted by anything strange, and once you go through the start and begin your round, you will need his undivided attention.

This short period in the ring before the start can be of great value to the rider too; it will give you the feel of the ring and you can double-check on any tight turns or angled approaches of which you should have made a mental note when walking the course. You will also be able to check any fences you might have seen the previous competitor knock and which may be slightly dislodged. This is really the responsibility of the arena party (known

Members of the Polish and German contingents walking the course of the Junior European individual championhip.

Marion Mould is in full control on Stroller one stride before take-off. It is impossible to fault Marion's position: the pony is full of impulsion and in a perfect position to jump the fence. Note how he has his hocks bent underneath him in order to push himself off the ground.

as the 'jump crew' in the United States), but they are only human and occasionally they slip up.

Paying attention to all these small details may well tip the balance between winning and losing a competition. With this in mind you may find it helpful to walk your course with an experienced rider, so never be afraid to ask. Nobody minds helping a youngster who is genuinely keen to learn. As you progress to a more advanced level of show jumping, the courses will become not only bigger but more technically demanding, and this study of the course beforehand becomes even more important. There will be no room for error on the part of horse or rider. In show jumping you get no second chance; one mistake and you are out of the running.

The rider must decide in advance how to ride each fence individually and the course as a whole, but he must also be prepared to change his mind in case of emergency. When pacing out the distance between two related fences

(fences are unrelated if they are more than 72 ft (22 m) apart; they become a combination fence if they are under 39 ft 4 in (12 m) apart) you should be able to decide exactly how many strides your horse will take and whether you will need to shorten or lengthen.

Some riders prefer not to count strides but just walk the distance to see whether it is long or short and then rely on their eye. It is certainly a great mistake to have it firmly fixed in your mind that you must take, say, four strides—so much depends on how your horse jumps the first element. If he does not make much ground over the first part and loses impulsion, you may have to shorten his stride and come through in five. But you must shorten immediately on landing. Here your reactions must be very quick and your horse instantly responsive; if you wait two strides and then decide to shorten, it will be too late. In a combination fence of course you are allowed no choice; any deviation from the number of strides intended is courting disaster and should only be attempted in dire emergency! With experience you will be able to tell exactly how a combination will ride, taking into consideration all the influencing factors—the structure of the fences involved, the state of the ground, the position of the fences in the ring, the gradient of the approach, etc.

Basically a combination fence needs to be approached with plenty of impulsion even if the distance is short. You will then find you have something up your sleeve in case of emergency. With any related distance, the way you jump the first fence is important and in a combination it becomes much more so. Impulsion is the energy formed by the harnessing of the horse's power by the rider. It must be maintained at all times throughout a show-jumping round but particularly when negotiating these related distances and combinations. You must maintain impulsion throughout changes of direction, especially when approaching a fence out of a corner or away from the collecting ring.

Do not confuse impulsion with speed—the two bear no relation to each other. Imagine the horse's body as a spring: impulsion is generated when the spring is compressed tightly, allowing for sufficient release of energy when required without uncoiling the spring to the extent of losing balance and momentum. A common fault in an inexperienced rider is to lose both pace and impulsion when shortening a stride. Any adjustments in stride

A good approach by Alwin Schockemöhle on Rex the Robber. Brilliant performer though he is, Rex the Robber does have a tendency to stop. Here, Alwin is avoiding this by pushing him forward with legs and weight while keeping a firm hold of his head to maintain impulsion in the approach. See how the horse's eye is looking back at the rider—a sign of unwillingness.

should be carried out without loss of pace, balance, or impulsion. Pace should only be varied according to the structure of the fence.

The perfect show-jumping round, then, should be smooth and fluent, without loss of balance or impulsion, and with the stride adjustments barely perceptible. Small wonder that there is only a small select band of show-jumping riders in the world who are capable of such artistry. Riders like David Broome, Frank Chapot, Rodney Jenkins, Alwin Schockemöhle and Eddie Macken—they make it look so deceptively easy. But unless we try to emulate them and aim at perfection, what chance have the rest of us?

Looking after your horse

10

I believe that most horses like jumping. To be successful a show jumper must enjoy his work or otherwise he will never stand up to the demands made of him. I'm certain the top horses sense that they are the stars of the stage, and they always seem to rise to a big occasion. It is an accepted fact that the evening sessions at Wembley, for instance, always produce better jumping than the afternoons, even when the same horses are jumping in both sessions. A good horse will always give a little extra when he senses an electric atmosphere and his adrenalin starts to flow.

However, like any actor, he must be allowed to relax between performances, otherwise he will become stale. This applies particularly to an international horse who is doing a lot of travelling and stabling in strange surroundings, but every show jumper needs a break from time to time. An hour or two turned out in the paddock each day is a good tonic and a quiet hack out in the country will freshen him up mentally. At the end of a long season he should be turned out in a field for a complete rest. With the popularity of indoor shows increasing, it is very tempting to keep a horse jumping all the year round, but he will not last very long as a result.

Weather permitting, your horse will benefit most from his holiday if you leave him out day and night so that he has a complete rest both physically and mentally. You may need to put a New Zealand rug on him in the really bad weather, and you must keep feeding him well. Hay alone is not sufficient to keep him warm, but as long as he has some good, hard, dry feed inside him, he should be able to stand all weathers.

A pleasant break from the tension of the show ring: Bouncer enjoys running free in the paddock.

You should allow yourself at least two months to get him fit again before the next season starts. During the first week of this period you should have him wormed and shod, and have the vet look at his teeth. Start with slow walking and jogging on good, level, firm ground and up and down hills. Road work is good for hardening a horse's legs. However, a show jumper's feet have to undergo a lot of jarring and I am not sure that too much road work does not add to the wear and tear. Equally, it is hard to find good ground in the middle of the winter, and a level road surface is infinitely preferable to ploughing through the mud. Make use of covered schools or indoor rings, if available, should the ground be too muddy or frozen.

Before the show season starts you will obviously have to do a little schooling over fences at home to tune up the horse both physically and mentally. With a young horse you will probably find you have to revert to some fairly elementary schooling as novices usually go back a bit after a rest, but he will soon progress again to the standard he reached at the end of the last season. A novice horse will therefore need much more jumping than an experienced one.

Most 'made' horses need very little jumping at home.

I'm a firm believer in saving their jumping for the show-ring. Every horse has only a limited working life in him and the more you jump him at home the shorter it will be. Once the show circuit has started, I don't believe it necessary to jump an experienced horse at home unless things should go wrong and you need to give him a school to restore his confidence. Obviously there are horses that need more jumping than others and will go better if they do some jumping at home the day before a show, but this all adds up to further stress and strain on their legs and feet.

A good knowledge of stable management, feeding and basic veterinary care is essential when caring for any horse. When you get to the stage of having a string of international jumpers to ride you will naturally have a groom to help you, but even so the rider still has to have the knowledge to supervise the feeding and general care of his horses. Furthermore, looking after and caring for the horse you ride undoubtedly increases the bond between you and strengthens your relationship.

The type of bedding you choose for your horse or pony will depend on a number of things, mainly your pocket, and his figure and wind. All things being equal, straw is probably the most practical. It is easy to obtain, to store, and to handle; it is clean and warm and provides good drainage. Wheat straw is the best, as barley straw is prickly, and horses tend to eat oat straw. In fact if you have a horse or pony which is inclined to put on too much weight, it is advisable to keep him off straw if possible and use sawdust or shavings. These make an excellent substitute but are not always easy to obtain. Shavings have an additional advantage if you have a horse which is thick in his wind or a permanent cougher. A bed of straw will be disastrous for such horses, but they rarely suffer on shavings. Another alternative is peat moss but personally I think this is inclined to get very damp and soggy, and it is hard to keep horses clean on it. Whatever your form of bedding, make sure that your horse has plenty to stand on during the day. There is nothing worse for his feet and legs than to stand on a hard cold surface for several hours a day.

Feeding is obviously of the utmost importance and everybody has his own special ideas on the subject. Each horse is an individual and must be fed as such. How you feed your particular horse will depend on his size, temperament and the amount of work he is doing. When you acquire a new horse never feed him too 'hot' to start with. It's a good idea to ask the horse's previous owner for advice. Some horses just cannot take any oats and if you make him unmanageable from the beginning you are in for trouble. When you have worked with him for a few days you will have some idea of his temperament and you can start giving him a little more if you think he needs it. It is all a matter of trial and error, but it is best not to start with the error! Basically, the good plain feeds—oats, bran and chaff—are the best, as with these you know exactly what your horse is getting. Horse pellets are convenient, but they can become very monotonous if fed on their own. To add interest you can give a little maize or soaked sugar beet, and carrots are a great treat and encourage a shy feeder. Always buy the highest quality as it is a false economy to buy second-rate feed. Give at least one damp feed a day, preferably at night; the easiest way to do this is to crumble the bran with hot water and mix it into the feed. You should be able to work out a correctly balanced diet for your horse using a diet sheet or with the advice of your local feed merchant, bearing in mind the ratio between phosphorus and calcium is 4 to 1. If you work on this basis you should get the maximum benefit from your different types of feed.

Your vet will tell you if your horse is lacking in any particular mineral, in which case you may need to feed one of the mineral supplements. It is best to feed that particular mineral in concentrate rather than one of the multi-mineral tonics. Salt is a necessary addition to a horse's feed and can be provided in the form of a salt lick. Water should always be available.

It is advisable to stick to regular feeding times if possible, but this is not always practical when away at shows. The number of feeds you give per day is a matter of personal choice and opinions vary too about when to give hay. Some leave a permanent supply of hay in the stable, others give a ration night and morning. I'm a firm believer in feeding plenty of chaff with the feed and giving a hay net only at night. Hay should be of the highest quality, hard and crisp and free from dust. It should smell sweet and not musty.

Grooming is the daily attention necessary to a stabled horse, not only to clean him but also to inspect him. If you groom him thoroughly every day you will immediately spot any cuts, swellings or lumps which might have

Above and above right:
Grooming is an essential part of
your daily routine, for cleaning
and inspecting your pony. It also
provides an ideal way of getting
to know your animal.

materialized. The actual cleaning process is vital to maintain condition of his skin and feet, when he is unable to lead his natural, free life exercising himself and rolling. The feet are probably the most important part of a show jumper's anatomy and it is essential that you look after these and oil them every day. Pick the foot out first and make sure that there is nothing hard or sharp lodged in it. Then oil the foot on the frog and the sole and all round the outside of the hoof. It is better to use a good-quality animal fat for this, rather than manufactured hoof oil. This keeps the frog and the hoof soft and replaces the natural oil taken out of the foot when shoeing. Check the shoes regularly; some horses' feet grow surprisingly quickly and need shoeing fairly frequently. Make sure there are no risen nails or clenches, and the shoes are firm and have not shifted. Before a show it is a good idea to check the stud holes. Clean out the screw thread with oiled cottonwool to avoid panic at the last moment.

Every rider should have at least some basic knowledge of veterinary care and a simple but well-equipped veterinary chest is an essential piece of your equipment. There is

Right: It is most important to
clean and oil your horse's feet
daily. Pay particular attention to
oiling the sole and the frog as
well as the outside of the hoof.
This is an important thing that a
lot of people overlook.

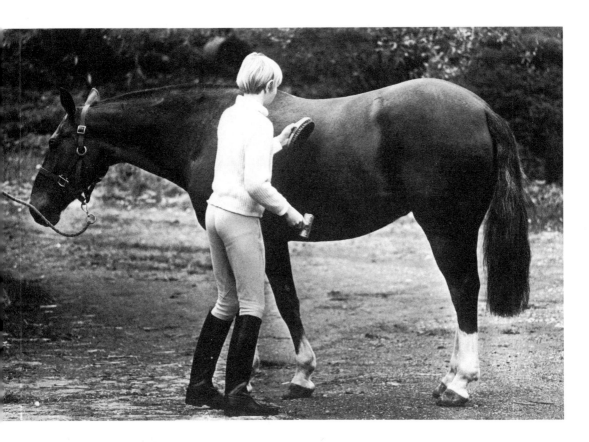

no need to fill it up with all sorts of fancy medicines and powders but these are some of the things you will need: thermometer, plenty of bandages, cottonwool, gamgee and Elastoplast, antibiotic dusting powder, and ointment for cuts and bruises; a tin of poultice, a tube of eye ointment, some cough mixture, a colic remedy and a packet of Epsom salts; some form of antibiotic injection to combat temperatures is also useful to have on hand, but *never* use a syringe unless you are fully competent. If ever you are in any doubt about your horse's well-being do not hesitate to call in your vet. It is extremely dangerous to try to diagnose or treat anything but a minor ailment yourself unless you have had considerable experience in this field. Whenever you have to call a vet do not be afraid to ask him questions—how he has made the diagnosis, what he prescribes for treatment, and why. If the treatment is fairly simple he may let you do it under his supervision.

Care of your tack is important, not only to keep it clean and in good condition but also to check it every day for any worn parts which might break. You should pay particular attention to stitching, as thread will wear out quicker than leather. It is advisable to move the buckles into different holes from time to time: with the cheek pieces on the bridle you can move them up one side and down the other side. Stirrup leathers can occasionally be cut shorter so that the weight from the stirrup comes in a different place. Never buy cheap saddlery—the best leather will last much longer, and it must fit perfectly and be a hundred per cent safe.

Travelling with horses safely and efficiently is something you will learn only from experience. But the most important consideration must always be the comfort of your horse. The miles you travel each season will increase in relation to the standard of your jumping, and when you are competing throughout the country or internationally as many juniors do these days, you will spend many long days and weeks travelling with your horse by road, rail, sea and air. In the USA and Australia the distances are vast by British standards, but travelling abroad to foreign coun-

Clean your tack regularly to keep it in good condition and to lessen the chance of any breakages.

tries presents its own problems with the inevitable red tape and seemingly unavoidable delays at the borders. It is rarely possible to take your horse out during these hold-ups so you must leave yourself enough room to be able to check on his blankets and rugs, bandages etc., and to be able to change them if necessary. Because of frequent changes of temperature, particularly when travelling by sea, it may be necessary to change his rugs two to three times in a day and it is a good idea to take his bandages off at the same time giving his legs a brisk rub before replacing them.

Bandages should be firm but never tight and should be put on over a large piece of gamgee or cottonwool with an even pressure all the way down from the knee or hock to the coronet. Be very careful not to fasten them too tight. There are on the market various kinds of knee boots and hock boots which give added protection, but these are

Make sure all your tack is correctly fitted before mounting.

During a long journey a horse's muscles will tend to stiffen up. A walk out on a halter will then help to relieve the stiffness and to relax him both physically and mentally.

inclined to rub if left on for any length of time. There is also a kind of foam-rubber-lined gaiter boot which can be used in place of bandages. These are very convenient in that they are quicker and easier to put on than bandages, but they do tend to become rather hot when travelling. A lightweight tail guard over the tail bandage will help to protect the tail from rubbing, but this too will need to be changed at intervals. A head guard is good protection.

Feeding and watering on these long trips should be little and often; most horses tend to lose their appetite somewhat when travelling and a small plain feed will be more appetizing than a large elaborate one. A light feed at fairly frequent intervals will help to relieve the boredom on a long journey as will a small hay net, but allowing your horse to stuff himself with unlimited hay you run the risk

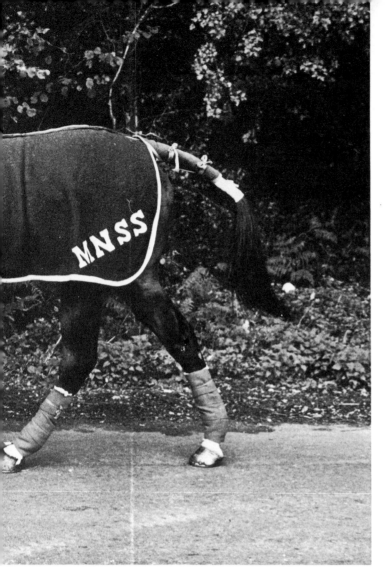

of colic. Probably you will be somewhat restricted as to how much you can take on these trips, and obviously you will not want to clutter your trailer or horse-box up with a lot of unnecessary luggage. However, you should be prepared for any emergency and it is much better to take too much than too little. Plenty of rugs for all weathers, together with any additional tack you might need, a spare set of horse shoes and a plentiful supply of feed, not forgetting your veterinary chest—these are your essentials. When you arrive at your destination, or if you are staying somewhere en route, a walk out in a halter, and if possible a nibble of grass, will freshen a horse up and ease the stiffness caused by long hours of travelling. If it is not too late at night, a quick grooming will make him feel good, and then you can leave him alone to rest and relax.

Travelling is fun - sometimes.

11

For many of you travelling will only involve quite shor distances near your home. But all along I have stressed how important it is to aim high, at the top. Being a successful show jumper, even as a junior, will these days involve quite a lot of travelling—and believe me, it is no always an enjoyable experience. I have had more than a taste of the excitements of travelling with horses. I hope this chapter will give you a glimpse of a side of show jumping the general public know very little about.

In all the years that Brian and I have been travelling with jumpers, I don't think we have had one single journey without some sort of dramatic incident or prolonged delay en route.

Flying is undoubtedly the quickest and easiest way to travel with horses, and they usually travel extremely well by air. Unfortunately, though, it is very expensive and the travel allowance one usually receives from the show is seldom enough to meet this cost. When travelling overland I find it much more convenient to take our own vehicle than to go by rail. At least it is possible to pack all the tack, feed and luggage into the truck and it stays there throughout the journey.

From the UK, of course, the Channel crossing itself very often presents its own problems, particularly when the weather is rough. It is no surprise when the captain refuses to risk horses on his ship if the wind is Force 5 or more, and sometimes the delay can be for days on end. You may then miss the first few days of a show or even lose the trip altogether. We have on occasions made a hectic dash from one port to another where the weather forecast is more hopeful, only to find the gale has got there before us! On the whole, I think it is best to stay where you are and hope for a change in the weather. There is so much red tape involving vet's papers, import documents, insurance cards, etc, that changing your intended route involves a vast amount of paperwork. At least while the delay is in your own country you should have no problems in finding temporary stabling, whereas if you are stuck in a foreign country, possibly running short of feed and not being able to speak the language, it is far more frustrating. It is on occasions like these that you are glad of the extra provisions that you happened to pack in case of emergency.

This has happened to Brian and me several times over the years, and I think the most exasperating occasion was after the Ostend show in Belgium in 1974. The show finished on the Sunday evening, and the horses were due to cross back to Dover that night. However, just as we arrived at the docks a gale started to blow up, heralding what proved to be one of the worst storms in the English Channel within living memory. The September Hickstead Meeting was due to begin on the following Thursday. It seemed impossible that the horses would not be back in time to jump there, but in fact they were delayed for nine

Junior show jumping at international level: The British squad parading before the Junior European Show Jumping Championships at Brussels in 1976. They came third, behind Switzerland and Ireland.

107

days and arrived in England the day after Hickstead finished!

Finding stabling on these occasions is always a problem, particularly as you have to be within a few miles of the docks in case of a sudden change in the weather. Some of the borders are closed to livestock overnight, and if you arrive after five o'clock you will have to stay there until the next morning. You are very rarely allowed to take a horse out of the horse-box due to quarantine regulations, but occasionally you may be lucky to find a farm nearby with a suitable cowshed. We were delayed coming back from Lucerne one year with Thou Swell, Spring Fever and a young horse called High Hopes. We were driving across France in the middle of the night, desperately looking for somewhere to get the horses out and give them a rest. My French is not very good at the best of times, but Brian's is non-existent, and as I became more exhausted and bad-tempered I found it increasingly difficult to make the French locals understand that we wanted overnight stabling for three horses. Eventually we found a farmhouse in a very rural village, seemingly miles from anywhere, and a farmer very kindly gave us the use of his cowbarn to tie the horses in. While Brian settled them in for what was left of the night, I began to cook bacon and eggs on our little portable gas stove in the back of the truck, and the farmer's family came out to watch. Soon we were surrounded by French villagers; seemingly word had got around and the entire population turned out to watch the strange foreigners eating bacon and eggs in the back of a horse-box!

At least when travelling in your own box you can stop when you feel like it, and you are entirely independent. Travelling by rail is all very fine if you can go straight to your destination on one train, but this is seldom possible. For some unknown reason it seems necessary to attach the horses to a different train every time they come into a station. This involves hours of shunting backwards and forwards and still more hours just sitting in sidings. The shunting is the worst, each tremendous bang nearly throwing the poor horses off their feet. After a while they get wise to it and you can see them listening to the approaching train and bracing themselves for the impact. While this shunting is going on you are never quite sure whether it is at last time for your train to move out of the station, or whether it is just being pulled onto another

rack. We would leap out to fill the horses' water-buckets, see the train link up and start to move off, dash back without our water only to stop again a few yards further up the line!

After one notorious trip to the Madrid show in June 965, the British team went on to Lisbon; I think it was ne of the most appalling journeys the horses have ever uffered by rail. It took the best part of a week to get to Madrid and then nearly five days on to Lisbon. Sir Mike Ansell (then Col. Mike), who, as many British readers will

An ideal way to relax during a long journey or between classes at a show. Horses love to roll in the sand and walking in the sea is the best treatment in the world for bruises, sore shins or filled legs. The photograph shows Bouncer about to roll on the beach at La Baule, in France.

know, has done more for modern show jumping than almost any other individual, and who was then Chairman of the B.S.J.A., heard about it and as usual immediately decided to do something about it. He flew out to Lisbon, heard all the details from those of us who travelled with the horses and then wrote a personal letter to General Franco, then Spanish president, complaining about the Spanish railways. On the way home, it was a different story. Our train was given an armed guard at either end, and went straight across the border and through Customs; the vets were ushered on board to check the papers and our documents stamped with the minimum delay. Col. Mike gave Brian a photostat copy of General Franco's reply, which was covered with a lot of official stamps and seals and looked very impressive. At any sign of trouble through Spain, Brian would wave it airily, and it produced a magical effect!

Undoubtedly the most dramatic journey we have ever had was on the way to a show in Milan, Italy, in October of the same year. This time we decided to take our own vehicle—with my three horses—Thou Swell, Spring Fever and a little chestnut thoroughbred called Dignity. Also going was Johnny Kidd. He was using the same travel agent, so we decided to go in convoy. It was arranged that we should drive across France into Switzerland as far as Brig. There the vans would be put on a goods train to go through the tunnel under the Swiss Alps. This is where the trouble started. There was a metal measuring device under which all vehicles had to drive to ensure there was room for them to go under the tunnel when loaded on the goods train. Unfortunately, the device was about level with our steering wheel and it was quite obvious that there was only room for a car to go underneath. According to the travel agent we had only two alternatives: to unload all our luggage and horses and put everything in a cattle truck on the back of the train, or to go approximately 300 miles further over the mountain pass. Remembering our recent experiences on trains, we chose the second alternative. It was only later that we heard that the pass was due to be closed for the winter to all traffic the following week!

All went well for the first couple of hours; it was a glorious day; the scenery was indescribably beautiful and it seemed much better than rattling along through a tunnel on the end of a train. However, as the slope grew steeper and the road became narrower and the bends sharper, the awful realization came to us that we weren't going to get to the top. We could see the road ahead of us winding up to the top of the mountain like a ribbon, and it disappeared into the clouds above the snow level. The bends became so sharp that a couple of times we had to reverse back towards the sheer drop to get round the corner. There was no way we could turn round, and yet as far as we could see there was no way we could go on. Furthermore, it was getting late and the sun was fast disappearing behind the mountain. I must admit I felt a rising sense of panic, and have never been more relieved than when we came to a small plateau which had been flattened out for use as a picnic area. There was no question of our going on, but Johnny Kidd, always one to accept a challenge, decided to have a go. He had only two horses and his truck had a much shorter wheelbase than ours, and he was able to negotiate bends without having to go into reverse. So we said goodbye to Johnny and Alec Sivell, who travelled with him, and made bets on who would be first to get to Milan.

We took our horses out to stretch their legs and have a bite of grass, and watched Johnny's van winding up and up the mountain until he disappeared into the clouds. He told us later that he got so scared looking out over the sheer precipice on one side that he sat on the floor of the cab all the way up, while Alec did the driving!

We then had to wind all the way back down to Brig and by the time we got there it was dark. There was a train leaving Brig in half an hour for Domodossola on the other side of the tunnel at the Italian border, so the agents found us a goods rail van and we transferred all three horses, together with our feed, tack, veterinary equipment and suitcases into it and left our own vehicle by the side of the road. The rail van had no partitions and we did not have time to improvise any, so all our gear was just thrown on the floor between the horses, and we opened a bale of hay for them to stand on. What is more, there was no lighting in the van and we couldn't find a torch or flashlight among the chaos. So as soon as we entered the tunnel we were in pitch darkness, with things falling about all over the floor, adding to the rattling and crashing noise of the train going through the tunnel. I shudder to think what might have happened if any of the horses had panicked, but luckily they were all amazingly calm. We sat at Domodossola all night and the next morning, with the usual shunting backwards and forwards to ensure that the

The 'lungeing yard' on the ship which the Australian team used to keep the horses fit on their way to England in 1960. The team won the gold medal in the Rome Olympics that year and the captain, Larry Morgan, who won the individual gold medal, is seen here lungeing one of their horses.

horses didn't rest, and eventually arrived in Milan about 6 pm. There was actually a road truck waiting to take us to the stables. The only snag was that it was too small to take three horses! After a further wait of two hours at the station in Milan, we were taken to the stables and as so often happens we found that they were straight stalls and not boxes. This is quite usual, as many of the continental horses are kept in stalls all the time, so whenever we go abroad we always take plenty of hammers and nails to convert the stalls into boxes. It is, however, an extremely frustrating and exhausting pastime at the end of a long journey. (Incidentally, Johnny arrived at the showground in one piece just two hours before we did!)

It is amazing how horses stand up to all these trials and tribulations and are still able to jump when they get to a show. It is fascinating, too, to see how a young horse gradually matures as he travels, and how even a nervous, highly strung horse will learn to take the most alarming experiences in his stride.

One of my first trips abroad was to Stockholm in 1962. We sailed from Harwich and we didn't take our truck, so the horses travelled in crates on one of the decks. Each horse was swung on board by crane in an open crate which looked as if it would fall to pieces at any moment. They stood with their heads looking over the side of the crate and could see the sea way below them as they swung perilously in mid-air. There was really no room for anyone to go with them, but Brian insisted and he managed to squeeze in with each horse just before take-off. I expected at any moment to see horses and husband plunging into the sea, but amazingly they stood quietly and all was well.

Unfortunately, accidents do sometimes happen. Peter Robeson had a horse called The Heron, which was dropped from a crane. It was in the days before it was obligatory to use a steel cable and the horse-crate was attached to the crane by a rope. The rope broke and the crate, complete with horse, fell about 20 ft (6 m) onto the deck. The horse broke several vertebrae in his neck and was out of action for a year, but it was a miracle that he was not killed.

When crossing the Irish Channel from Holyhead to Dublin, horses are led onto the boat down a ramp and into the cattle-hold below. The steepness of the ramp depends on the state of the tide, but this method is much better than swinging them on with cranes.

When Brian travelled to England with the Australian three-day event team horses in 1960, the ship was fully equipped with large boxes and a lungeing area. The team spent about five weeks on the ship and obviously they wanted the horses fairly fit on arrival in England, so as soon as they left Sydney they built a small exercise area on the deck with a passageway leading from the stables. They put a large tarpaulin on the floor and up over the wooden rails which formed the walls, and covered it with straw and sand. Each horse was exercised every day on the lunge, apart from just two days when it was too rough to risk

113

taking them out. In fact, they even had a fair bit of hill work to get them fit, as with the continuous swell of the sea they were going uphill one minute and down the next!

Flying is undoubtedly the most practical and the least tiring way to travel horses, although this too can have its hair-raising moments. Horses have on rare occasions had to be destroyed when panicking and going berserk in an aeroplane, and thus endangering lives.

Another horse of Peter Robeson's, the famous Firecrest, actually put his foot through the fuselage of a plane going home from Rotterdam one year. In this case the space for the horses was somewhat restricted and the stalls were very narrow. A lot of horses suffer from a sort of claustrophobia when enclosed in a tight space, and they start to panic and climb the partitions. Firecrest kicked one hind foot through the metal of the fuselage and the more he struggled the more it became entangled. It wasn't until the plane landed that the leg could be cut free. By some miracle of veterinary skill and patient nursing the horse was saved and able to jump again the following season.

In 1962, I took my two horses to Madrid for the European Ladies' Championship with Pat Smythe. We flew in an old Bristol Freighter and we had to stop off at Rotterdam to pick up a Dutch girl, Tineke Zwolsman, and her two horses. Unfortunately, we all appeared to have rather too much luggage and the pilot refused to take off until we discarded some of it. Naturally, none of us wanted to leave anything behind, but after several hours of arguing we left a small amount of feed at the airport. However, the plane was still considerably overweight and it seemed to be travelling down the runway for an eternity before it finally took off. I hate flying anyway and I was convinced that my last moment had come.

Coming home after the show we had to send most of the luggage on another plane. Only Brian and Paula, Pat's girl, were allowed with the horses. The airport at Madrid was at a higher altitude, the runway was shorter than at Rotterdam, and the pilot reckoned that with the full load he wouldn't have got the plane off the ground.

Of course, carrying horses in one of the big planes specially equipped to take up to as many as twenty-four horses is the ideal way to travel. Brian flew out with the British horses for the Olympic games in Montreal in 1976. In fact, he had an interest in two of them as he trained Hugh Thomas and Playamar for the three-day event

Loading up the horses for the British team's journey to the 1976 Montreal Olympics.

team, and our own Bouncer was in the show-jumping team. They had a perfect flight both going over and coming back; the pilot was extremely sympathetic to the horses and everything for once went without a hitch. There were seventeen show jumpers, eventers, and dressage horses on board, and they all travelled extremely well. The take-off and landing were so smooth as to be almost imperceptible, and the only sign of excitement from the horses on the whole journey was a whinny from two or three as the plane touched down. The horses travelled in large crates, two abreast, on one side of a passageway running the full length of the plane. The one slightly anxious moment came when unloading; Bouncer put his head up as he backed out, so pulling off his halter and bridle on the roof of the crate. He just stood there in the middle of Montreal Airport with nothing on! Luckily, the travel agents insist on building a temporary enclosure all round the plane in case of just such an emergency, and all was well. In the unlikely, but very undesirable, event of a horse getting loose at one of the big airports, all the air traffic would have to be held up, and the insurance coverage has to run to several million pounds (or dollars —depending where you are!).

A great life

12

Peeople often ask Brian and me if we want our children to carry on the family tradition of show jumping; well, I suppose the honest answer would be 'yes'. Show jumping has given me so much.

There is a very close relationship among the show-jumping fraternity. You travel the world; meet up in different places and share the same experiences, the same thrills and disappointments. Even if you drop out of the sport for a few years, as I did after the days of Thou Swell and Spring Fever, while I was having my two children, you come back to find that the life hasn't changed. There are plenty of new faces, of course, as more and more people are coming into the sport each year, but most of the old ones are still around and it seems as if you have never been away.

Show jumping is a way of life, something that really gets into your blood. Of course, it has its drawbacks. People who think this is a glamorous sport would be astonished if they realized the tremendous amount of hard work involved, the long tiring hours, the often very uncomfortable and unpleasant conditions that we have to put up with. It is only the end-product as seen by millions of spectators in person or on television which is glamorous. Behind the scenes are the very unglamorous realities—the hours spent cleaning mud off your horse and tack when you come home late after a wet show; sitting up all night with a sick horse; the long, often nightmarish hours of travelling; arriving at a show in the middle of the night in pouring rain and finding your stables are flooded out, or that someone else has taken possession of them. This side of the life requires tremendous dedication, determination and self-discipline—all very good for the character!

Working with horses demands endless patience and self-control, while experience in the ring teaches you to be a good competitor. It also helps to develop your willpower and concentration. Your powers of concentration will play an important part in your success, both before and during a competition and while schooling at home. You must be able to feel exactly how your horse is going and what sort of mood he is in. Horses are like humans: they have their good days and their bad ones. It is up to you to decide the amount of work you should give him, not only when you ride him at home, but also when warming up for a show.

I always like to be on my own during the time leading up to an important competition. You have to tune yourself mentally to a big event and concentrate on a thousand small details: how your horse is going, when to give him a practice jump, how the course is riding, which distances are long or short, which fences are likely to cause trouble and, perhaps most important of all, the course itself. Every rider takes the wrong course from time to time, but it is nevertheless a very frustrating and annoying experience. This attention to detail is an important part of the preparation for the competition ahead, and there is

Keeping it going in the family: The author and her son with Bouncer.

nothing more distracting than being interrupted by some-body who is in no way connected with show jumping. I am sure a lot of the young autograph-hunters think the riders are snooty and superior when they refuse to sign auto-graphs at such a time, but competitors do have other things to think about.

Total concentration is even more essential during your actual round, and once you go through the start the fences come up so quickly there is no time to let your attention wander for an instant. Your reactions must be immediate and your horse instantly responsive.

I am often asked what it is like to jump in front of millions of television viewers. Well, the answer is the riders don't give it a thought any more than they notice the

Two moments at the 1976 Junior European Show Jumping Championships. Brian Macmahon of Ireland, the individual Champion, riding Heather Honey (opposite) and John Brown of England, on Paddy Connelly (above).

crowds of spectators. Once you are in that ring your mind should be completely oblivious to anything else. In the British Jumping Derby of 1976, a photographer walked across a fence just as I was coming into it and I yelled at him to get out of the way. I certainly didn't stop to think that there was a television microphone just beside the fence and I had no idea what I said. I always think it a bit tactless of the engineers to place their microphones in such unfortunate positions!

Of course, young children find it very hard to concentrate on any one thing for very long. Our daughter made us laugh when riding in her first competition, a Minimus Pony Club Hunter Trial. Brian and I were taking it in turns to run along beside her in case of accidents. She got

119

about half-way round the course and was coming into a small log fence. When she was about four strides away she turned round to Brian and said, 'They haven't even announced my name yet!' After another couple of fences, I took over from Brian and she said, 'Mummy, a photographer took a super photo of me over that last jump.' She obviously didn't have her mind fully on the job.

It is amazing how horses too will develop their powers of concentration with experience. A young novice horse is very easily distracted by everything around him, and very often fails even to see a fence in front of him; but it takes something very out of the ordinary to divert the attention of an experienced horse from his job. This was demonstrated in an amazing way by my mare, Spring Fever, in the Nations' Cup in Rotterdam in 1965. A large Dalmatian dog ran into the ring as we were coming into the first fence. He ran round us in circles, barking his head off and somehow managing to appear in front of us on both the take-off and the landing side of each fence. I think in a normal competition I would have pulled up, as I was certain that the mare would have a bad fall, but in a Nations' Cup you just can't retire. Anyway, to her eternal credit we finished the round, complete with dog, with a total of only four faults. The extraordinary thing was that not once did Spring Fever show any sign of even noticing the dog's presence—a true professional.

When you are travelling abroad by invitation of an international show or as a member of a team, the show usually provides first-class hotel accommodation for its competitors. Nearer home, however, nearly all show-jumping riders live either in caravans (known as campers in America) or specially equipped horse vehicles when they are staying at a show. In the evening when the lights come on in all these temporary homes, the stable area becomes quite a little social community. The riders and their families, the owners, the grooms, all get together over endless cups of coffee and talk about the day's results, the courses, the current form, and the prospects for tomorrow. This is the time to analyse your day's work and to decide how you can improve upon it. In the general discussion you will usually learn something, and on reflection you may be able to see why a particular fence came down or where you could have saved a couple of seconds. Very few riders, however brilliant, come out of the ring satisfied that they have jumped a perfect round.

There is always room for improvement. I think it is this continual urge to do better next time that makes the sport so fascinating.

Yes, it's a great life. Of course you will have your share of disappointments and frustrations, like losing a competition you desperately wanted to win by a fraction of a second, or having the last fence down, or a foot in the water—just a matter of inches between brilliant success and miserable failure. You may have your best horse going lame or sick before an important show, or even the tragedy of losing a favourite horse. But the compensations and rewards are infinite, from the joy of receiving your very first rosette, to the pride of being selected to represent your country, the thrill and excitement of helping your team to win a Nations' Cup; from the quiet satisfaction of producing a good performance from a young horse you have made yourself, to the sheer exhilaration of achieving a clear round over a really severe and difficult course. These treasured moments you will re-live over and over again for the rest of your life and this is what makes it all so worthwhile.

Basic rules
and useful addresses

While most people interested in show jumping will know something of the basic rules, there may be some of you who are unfamiliar with the method of scoring in a competition, the various classes available to the different grades of horses, and so on. Only the basics are given here; whether you live in Britain the USA or Australia, the best way to find out about the details is to write to your national federation for a copy of their rules. Some addresses are given at the end of this section.

The F.E.I. (Fédération Equestre Internationale) methods for judging have now been adopted by most of the national federations, and the B.S.J.A and E.F.A. rules vary only slightly in such details as the permitted use of saddlery.

Basically the method of scoring for a normal competition in Britain is as follows: for the first disobedience in a round, 3 faults; for the second disobedience in a round, 6 faults; for the third disobedience in a round, elimination; for knocking a fence down (this includes altering the height or the spread of an obstacle, or knocking over a ring or support), 4 faults; fall of horse and/or rider, 8 faults; for exceeding the time allowed, ½ fault for each second or part of a second; for exceeding the time limit (which is twice the 'time allowed'), elimination.

There are certain competitions which have their own rules of scoring, where faults are penalised by time, or when points are scored for fences cleared.

There are several other faults for which the penalty is elimination. The most common of these are as follows: taking the wrong course, starting before the signal, positively showing an obstacle to your horse, napping or disobedience during the course of a round for more than 60 seconds, failing to go through the start within 45 seconds of the signal, horse or rider leaving the ring during the course of a round, unauthorised outside assistance, knocking over the timing apparatus, entering or leaving the ring without the judges' permission.

Timing is used in all competitions where possible, and the bigger shows use automatic apparatus. The time allowed for any competition depends on the length of the course, and on the Table, or Bareme, under which the competition is being judged.

Most countries have some sort of grading system for their horses and ponies. On the continent of Europe jumpers are very often graded according to their age. In Australia they are graded on the number of outright wins, and in the USA and Great Britain on the amount of prize money won. Under B.S.J.A. rules there are three grades of horse, C, B, and A, the lowest grade being C, while the ponies have just two grades, JC and JA.

There are several classes for novice horses restricted to those which have won well under the limit in their grade, such as the

'Foxhunter' and 'Junior Foxhunter' competitions. These provide a good introduction to the show ring for the novice as the courses are considerably lower and more straightforward than in the Grade C classes.

For the rider who is graduating from junior to senior classes there are various 'Young Riders' classes which provide a good stepping stone. These are usually open to any grade of horse.

While some competitions are restricted to one particular grade, others cater for two grades at once—'B and C' or 'A and B'—and an 'Open' competition is open to any grade.

The 'Popular Open' classes, both junior and senior, are useful for the young pony or horse which has recently upgraded, and also for those which are not quite good enough for the top grade. These are restricted to ponies and horses which have won less than a certain sum of prize money during the current or the previous season.

Aside from the ordinary jump-off classes there are several competitions which are ideal for a horse which has just upgraded. In the 'Accumulator Competition' the course is made up of seven or eight single fences, increasing in value and severity. This gives you a chance to jump some bigger fences without the risk of getting into trouble in combinations. The 'Puissance' can serve the same purpose, but you must be prepared to withdraw after one or two rounds to avoid overfacing your horse. I am against this class in principle because I think it is wrong to keep asking a horse to jump higher and higher until he is beyond his limit.

The Bareme A classes (A.H.S.A. Table II, Sec. 1) which are judged on faults and time are a good introduction to jumping bigger courses against the clock. In the event of equality of faults time decides the winner, but a steady clear round will beat a fast 'four faults' as long as there are no time faults. Very often these classes are held as secondary competitions in the Main Ring at the big shows, and they provide a valuable opportunity to introduce your young horse to the big time.

In the Bareme C classes (A.H.S.A. Table III) the courses are smaller and these are judged on time alone, with seconds added for each fence down. These competitions are not good for young horses as speed has more influence on the result than jumping.

The Top Score or Gambler's Competition gives you a choice of fences of various degrees of difficulty. With a novice horse you can sometimes pick out an easy course over the smaller fences, but in this type of competition the fences are usually placed at awkward angles and distances from one another, and this is not a good idea for the novice.

One type of competition which I think can be of great value to a young horse is the 'Six Bar'. Unfortunately this event seems to have fallen from favour lately, and is not very often included in the show schedules. The course consists of six upright obstacles in a straight line with only two strides (about 11 metres) between them. The obstacles may all be of the same height, but are usually of progressive heights. As in the use of your jumping lanes at home this competition provides very good physical and mental exercise for a young horse. It can also be quite a strain on him as the fences are raised after each round, and a horse must use great physical effort and concentration to clear the six fences in a row. For this reason it is advisable to withdraw after two or three rounds.

The rules of American show jumping run along very similar lines. Jumper classes are scored according to either of two A.H.S.A. tables.

Touch classes are under Table I, as follows: for touching an obstacle with any portion of the horse's body behind the stifle, ½ fault; for touching an obstacle with any portion of the horse's body in front of the stifle, with any part of the rider or his equipment, or touching flags, standards, or timers, 1 fault; for knocking down an obstacle, or placing one or more feet in the water or on the marking strip of a water jump, 4 faults; for the second cumulative disobedience, 6 faults; for the third cumulative disobedience, fall of a horse and/or rider, jumping fences out of order, and several other procedural mistakes, elimination.

'Knockdown' classes are scored under Table II, in which faults and eliminations are identical to Table I except that touches are not penalized, nor is a fall of a horse or rider.

Classes in the Junior Division are categorized as follows: Preliminary, for horses that have not won at least U.S. $1000 (£1750); Intermediate, $1000 to $3000 (£1750-£5250); Open, in excess of $3000 (£5250); and Amateur-Owner irrespective of winnings, a horse exhibited by its amateur owner or an amateur member of the owner's immediate family. Generally speaking, courses are less demanding for Preliminary and Amateur-Owner jumpers.

Junior Jumper Division classes' eligibility, scoring, and physical requirements are based on the Senior Jumping Division, except that fences' heights and spreads are to a maximum of 5ft (1.52m).

For detailed guidance about rules, write to your national federation for their up-to-date rule book. For this purpose and for general information of any kind, the following addresses will be useful:

Fédération Equestre Internationale, Avenue Hamoir 38, Brussels 18, Belgium.

British Show Jumping Association, National Equestrian Centre, Stoneleigh, Warwickshire CV8 2LR, England.

British Equestrian Federation, National Equestrian Centre, Stoneleigh, Warwickshire CV8 2LR, England.

American Horse Shows Association, 527 Madison Avenue, New York, N.Y., U.S.A.

United States Equestrian Team, Inc., Gladstone, N.J. 07934, U.S.A.

Equestrian Federation of Australia, Royal Show Ground, Epsom Road, Ascot Vale, 3032, Australia.

The Pony Club of Great Britain, National Equestrian Centre, Stoneleigh, Warwickshire CV8 2LR, England.

U.S. Pony Clubs, 303 South High Street, West Chester, Pennsylvania 19380, U.S.A.

Books to read

General

The Complete Book of Show Jumping edited by Michael Clayton and William C. Steinkraus (Heinemann, London, and Crown, New York) covers all aspects of show jumping, including training, course-building, and famous horses and riders.

Show Jumping: Officers' Hobby Into International Sport by Pamela Macgregor-Morris (David & Charles, Newton Abbot) gives a history of show jumping and its personalities.

Encyclopedia of Show Jumping and Combined Training by Charles Stratton (Robert Hale, London).

Show Jumping Down Under by Ted Dwyer (Robert Hale) gives an account of show jumping in Australia and New Zealand.

Riding High by Col. Sir Mike Ansell (Peter Davies, London) is a complete guide to show jumping, from choosing a horse and training, to designing a course and its obstacles.

The U.S. Equestrian Team Book of Riding edited by William C. Steinkraus (Simon & Schuster, New York). Olympic riders and coaches present a mixture of reminiscences and advice.

So You're Showing Your Horse by David A. Spector (Arco, New York) covers all steps in procedure, from sending in entry forms to shipping out of the show grounds.

Training—American books

Hunt Seat Equitation by George H. Morris (Doubleday, New York). The author, former American Olympic rider and leading trainer of juniors, outlines the training of a hunter or jumper horse.

Riding and Jumping by William C. Steinkraus (Doubleday, New York and Pelham, London). The Olympic gold medallist focuses on his personal approach to the sport.

Showing Your Horse by Harlan C. Abbey (Arco, New York) contains training and competition techniques gleaned from Rodney Jenkins, David Kelley, and other top American riders.

Horsemanship by Waldemar Seunig (Doubleday, New York and Robert Hale, London). This, and the following two books, give somewhat technical discussions of elementary and advanced dressage.

The Complete Training of Horse and Rider by Alois Podhajsky (Doubleday, New York, and Harrap, London).

Dressage for Beginners by R. V. L. ffrench Blake (Houghton Mifflin, Boston).

Training—British and Australian books

The Trainers by Ann Martin (Stanley Paul, London) discusses world-famous show jumping trainers and their riding techniques.

The Essentials of Horsemanship by E. Hartley Edwards (Ward Lock, London) presents a comprehensive survey of riding and horsemanship.

Better Show Jumping by Lt.-Col. W. Froud (Kaye & Ward, London) gives advice on training and jumping skills.

Training Explained and *Jumping Explained* by Carol Green (Ward Lock, London). Both give practical advice in easy-to-follow terms on training techniques for horse and rider.

Technical terms

A.H.S.A. American Horse Shows' Association.

Affiliated Associated with or recognized by a national federation (as in 'affiliated show').

Aids The signals by which the rider communicates his intentions to the horse.

Arena party Party of helpers known in the US as the jump crew. They help the course-builder build the course, and replace fences that are knocked down.

B.S.J.A. British Show Jumping Association.

Backing off The action of a horse which voluntarily slows up, dropping the bit and losing impulsion, when approaching a fence.

Bareme International term for a set, or table, of rules applicable to a competition.

Bascule The action of a horse rounding himself over a jump—from the French 'basculer' (to see-saw).

Bell boot *See* Over-reach boot.

Brushing boot Boot worn on the front or back legs between the knee and the fetlock joint to protect a horse from 'brushing' the legs against one another.

Cadence Regulated rhythm.

Cavalletti Small wooden jump used in schooling horses.

Chute *See* Jumping lane.

Class Competition.

Clench Tip of a horse-shoe nail which comes through the hoof.

Collecting ring The area on a show ground where competitors assemble before a class.

Combination Series of jumps numbered as one fence, and separated by distances of 39 ft 4 in (12.00 m) or less.

Conformation Physical build or make-up of a horse.

C.S.I.O. Concours de Saut International Officiel (international official jumping show).

Double Combination consisting of two jumps

Dressage Training of a horse, on the flat, in obedience and deportment.

E.F.A. Equestrian Federation of Australia.

F.E.I. Fédération Equestre Internationale show jumping's international governing body.

Fetlock joint The leg joint below a horse's knee.

Flexion Bend.

Forehand The part of a horse in front of the rider.

Frog Fleshy cushion in the sole of a horse's hoof.

Gamgee Gauze lined with cottonwool, used inside bandages.

Ground line Positive visible line at the base of a jump.

Gymnastic work Muscular exercise.

Hock Joint in horse's hind leg between the stifle and the fetlock joint.

Hors concours Literally 'outside the competition'—a term used when a rider jumps round without being an actual competitor.

Horse box Horse-carrying road vehicle. 'Horse van' is the nearest American term.

Impulsion Driving force from the horse's hindquarters which drives it forward.

Irons Stirrups.

Jump crew *See* Arena party.

Jumping lane Series of schooling jumps at related distances, usually enclosed by a wall or fence; known in the US as a 'chute'.

Jump-off Round to decide the winner of a competition from competitors tying for first place in a previous round.

Loins Part of a horse's body behind the saddle on each side of the spine.

Loose-box Stable in which horses can be left

loose, and not tied as in stalls.

Lunge To walk a horse in circles on the end of a long rein.

Nations' Cup Official international team jumping competition held only at a C.S.I.O.

Near Left (as in 'near side').

Off Right (as in 'off side').

Over-bitting Putting too severe a bit in a horse's mouth.

Over-reach boot Rubber boot worn round the horse's foot to protect against over-reaching, that is knocking the front and back feet together.

Parabola Trajectory, or curved line, followed by a horse in the air over a jump.

Placing-pole Pole laid on the ground in front of a jump to ensure a correct take-off.

Poling Banging a horse's legs with a pole to make him jump higher. This is the American term; it is known in Britain as 'rapping'.

Poll Top of a horse's head between the ears.

Puissance Type of show jumping competition designed purely to test a horse's ability to jump heights.

Quarters Part of the horse behind the rider.

Rapping *See* Poling.

Stall Compartment in a stable in which a horse is tied up and unable to turn round.

Table *See* Bareme.

Three Day Event Competition held normally over three days which includes three phrases—dressage, cross-country, and show jumping.

Treble Combination consisting of three jumps.

Unbroken Term used of horses which have not yet been broken in.

Picture acknowledgements

Permission to reproduce photographs has kindly been given by the following:

Rex Coleman: 61, 62 (both), 64, 86; *Daily Express:* 116; Findlay Davidson: 30, 60, 71 (both), 72, 75, 76, 78, 80, 92, 93, 95, 106, 118, 119; C. Delcourt: 63 (top); Richard Earle: 69; Leigh Francis: 109; Clive Hiles: 15, 63 (bottom), 66, 87, 88, 91; E. D. Lacey: 14, 41 (both), 65, 81; Leslie Lane: 25, 83; Sport and General Press Agency, London: 115; John Taylor: 77; W. D. & H. O. Wills, photograph by R. M. Knutsen: 84.

The following photographs were specially taken for the book by E. D. Lacey: 2, 6, 12, 16, 17 (all), 18-19, 20, 21, 22, 26, 27 (both), 28, 32 (both), 33 (both), 34, 35, 37, 42, 43, 45, 46-47, 48, 50, 51, 52, 53, 54 (all), 55, 56 (both), 57, 58 (both), 59, 85, 96, 100, 101 (both), 102, 103, 104-5.

Line drawings by Hilary Evans.

Index